GREEN LEDGERS:

Case Studies

in Corporate

Environmental

Accounting

WORLD
RESOURCES
INSTITUTE

May 1995

Edited by

Daryl Ditz
Janet Ranganathan
R. Darryl Banks

Contributors

Beth Beloff
Miriam Heller
Devaun Kite
Ajay Maindiratta
David Shields
Christopher Stinson
Rebecca Todd

Library of Congress Cataloging-in-Publication Data

Green ledgers : case studies in corporate environmental accounting /
  edited by Daryl Ditz, Janet Ranganathan, Darryl Banks.
      p. cm.
    Includes bibliographical references.
    ISBN 1-56973-032-6
      1. Industrial management—Environmental aspects—United
States—Case studies. 2. Environmental auditing—United States—
Case studies. I. Ditz, Daryl W. II. Ranganathan, Janet, 1962–
III. Banks, Darryl, 1950–
HD30.255.G74   1995
658.4'08—dc20   95-18773
                                                                      CIP

Kathleen Courrier
Publications Director

Brooks Belford
Marketing Manager

Hyacinth Billings
Production Manager

Lomangino Studio
Cover Design

Each World Resources Institute report represents a timely, scholarly treatment
of a subject of public concern. WRI takes responsibility for choosing the study
topics and guaranteeing its authors and researchers freedom of inquiry. It also
solicits and responds to the guidance of advisory panels and expert reviewers.
Unless otherwise stated, however, all the interpretation and findings set forth in
WRI publications are those of the authors.

CONTENTS

FOREWORD

From the board room to the shop floor to the marketplace, business decisions are skewed when environmental costs are hidden. Common accounting practices hide these costs in two ways: by burying them in "nonenvironmental" accounts and by failing to link costs to the activities that spawn them. As a result, managers are forced to make crucial business decisions—what products to manufacture, what technologies to employ, and what materials to use— without command of all the relevant facts. Now, more than ever, these managers are on the line as regulation, public concern, and corporate commitments make it increasingly important to account for environmental costs.

The good news is that hidden in the shadows of the information failure created by conventional business accounting practices are unexploited opportunities to increase profits, use materials more efficiently, and protect the environment. What's more, firms of any size and in any industrial sector can make such gains, given the accurate cost information that evolving environmental accounting practices provide.

Green Ledgers: Case Studies in Corporate Environmental Accounting—edited by Daryl Ditz, associate in WRI's Technology Program; Janet Ranganathan, research analyst; and R. Darryl Banks, program director—offers an insider's view of corporate environmental accounting. It is not about the information that firms report to the EPA or even to their stockholders, but about the information they gather for their own purposes and how they use it. To explore how different firms handle this task, WRI—together with teams of academic researchers and corporate staff—studied nine companies, including Amoco Oil, Ciba-Geigy, Dow Chemical, Du Pont, and S.C. Johnson. Derived from in-depth interviews and confidential information, the case studies demonstrate how a better accounting of environmental costs leads to better business decisions—critical since firms must continually look for ways to squeeze more product out of less raw material and energy.

What did the participating corporations learn about their own practices? For openers, once the case study teams teased environmental costs out of the sundry accounts they had been hidden in, the sum could be astounding. Du Pont, for instance, found that environmental costs accounted for more than 19 percent of the total manufacturing cost of one agricultural pesticide. Relying only on conventional accounting practices, managers might never have known. Other companies made similar discoveries.

More important, the case studies in *Green Ledgers* describe how companies can use environmental cost information to improve profitability and reduce environmental risk. For instance, managers at Heath Tecna, a composite materials manufacturer, found that by changing their production processes they make materials use more efficient, reduce hazardous waste generation, and reduce costs. At Cascade Cabinet, a decision to switch from nitrocellulose lacquer—a hazardous material and source of air pollution—to a more benign varnish cut manufacturing costs significantly. A better understanding of environmental costs can also affect pricing decisions: when Dow Chemical faced a stark choice between shutting down a product line or investing in cleaner technology, its industrial customers accepted slightly higher prices in return for a guaranteed supply of the product.

As befits a book about an emerging discipline that is edging toward the mainstream, *Green Ledgers* contains a how-to guide for introducing environmental accounting. Managers who want to reap its benefits will appreciate the authors' practical advice about how to launch a pilot project, identify environmental costs, and integrate these activities into ongoing business processes.

As the authors note, environmental accounting is not just about generating information, but also about putting companies on a track to being leaner and greener. This form of accounting makes it possible to hold managers accountable for the environmental costs of their decisions—no matter where in the firm these play out. Environmental accounting must become part of strategic planning and capital budgeting exercises, not a free-standing effort. This means infusing core business thinking with accurate perceptions of environmental costs.

The case studies and analyses set forth in *Green Ledgers* complement the findings and recommendations presented in such WRI studies as *Jobs, Competitiveness, and Environmental Regulation: What are the Real Issues?*, *Beyond Compliance: A New Industry View of the Environment*, and *Transforming Technology: An Agenda for Environmentally Sustainable Growth in the Twenty-first Century*. Although *Green Ledgers* takes aim mostly at a business audience, academics, professional associations, and even regulators can use it to promote better environmental accounting on the part of the private sector. As the next step in its focus on business decision-making, WRI's Technology and Environment program is exploring indicators of environmental performance that firms can use to drive and evaluate their progress toward cleaner technology.

We would like to express our appreciation to The Hitachi Foundation, The Moriah Fund, Inc., and the U.S. Environmental Protection Agency for their financial support of the research presented in *Green Ledgers*. We would also like to thank the nine companies that made this pioneering study possible by opening their doors and their books to our authors. To our financial backers and our corporate collaborators alike, we owe a debt of gratitude.

Jonathan Lash
President
World Resources Institute

ACKNOWLEDGMENTS

We would like to thank the many colleagues and friends who contributed to this project. In particular, we are grateful to the participating firms and their representatives who made the case studies possible. It would be impossible to list all those who participated, but we are especially appreciative of Kristine Link and Neal Thurber (Amoco), John Earle (Cascade Cabinet), George Muhlebach (Ciba-Geigy), Carol Ashley (Dow Chemical), Ray Anderson (Du Pont), Brian Anderson (Eldec), Roy Chandler (Heath Tecna), Jane Hutterly (S.C. Johnson), and Lance Brittain and Marlin Trigg (Spectrum Glass).

We are indebted to Dr. Delwin Roy, President of the Hitachi Foundation, for their generous support and for his interest and encouragement throughout this project. We are also very grateful to the Moriah Fund and the U.S. Environmental Protection Agency for their financial support.

We appreciate the very helpful comments we received on drafts of this manuscript from Corrine Boone and Ali Khan (Ontario Hydro), Marc Epstein (Stanford University), Randy Price (J.M. Huber), Laurie Regelbrugge (The Hitachi Foundation), Allen White (Tellus Institute), Alan Willis (Willis Associates), Pieter Winsemius (McKinsey & Company); and at WRI Alan Brewster, Nina Kogan, Jonathan Lash, Walt Reid, Bob Repetto, and Dan Tunstall. Thanks to Dan Abbasi for his initial efforts on this project. Thanks as well to the members of the Advisory Panel, including David Kling (EPA), James Maxwell (MIT), Bruce Smart, Allen White (Tellus Institute), and Jeannie Wood (AT&T).

We would also like to thank Kathleen Courrier, Hyacinth Billings, Linda Starke, and Robbie Nichols for their skill and dedication in producing this publication. Finally, a special thanks to Valerie Williams and Jennifer Thorne for their many efforts during this project.

D.D.
J.R.
R.D.B.

I.

ENVIRONMENTAL ACCOUNTING: AN OVERVIEW

By Daryl Ditz, Janet Ranganathan, and R. Darryl Banks

A. Environmental Accounting Inside the Firm

1. Background

Environmental limits don't simply constrain business. Rather, companies are finding, environmental considerations increasingly infuse everything from product design to marketing, from purchasing to product stewardship, from employee relations to executive compensation. Now the challenge for corporations is to fully integrate environmental thinking into corporate decision-making—to, in other words, translate their environmental concerns into the language of business.

Environmental costs are dispersed throughout most businesses and can appear long after decisions are made. Unfortunately, conventional accounting practices—developed to serve financial reporting requirements—rarely illuminate environmental costs or stimulate better environmental performance. Managerial accounting's traditional dependence on discrete, historical transactions and the common practice of pooling overhead costs can conceal and distort critical information on environmental and other costs.

Not only achievable, better accounting for environmental costs is crucial to long-term business sustainability. This book examines actual practices in nine companies. *(See Table 1.)* Case studies of these businesses provide fresh insights into how firms account for environmental costs and show that, even where environmental costs are sizable, they are often systematically underappreciated.

Table 1. Participating Companies

Amoco Corporation

Sales	$10.8 billion (refined products)
Employees	47,000
Business	Crude Oil Production, Processing, Marketing and Distribution, Petrochemicals
Case Focus	Yorktown Refinery (Chapter II)

Ciba-Geigy

Employees	92,000
Business	Diversified Pharmaceuticals, Specialty Chemicals and Agricultural Products
Case Focus	Chemical Additive (Chapter III)

Dow Chemical

Sales	$18 billion
Employees	61,000
Business	Diversified Chemicals, Plastics, Pharmaceuticals, Agricultural Products, and Consumer Products
Case Focus	Polymer-based Coating (Chapter IV)

E.I. Du Pont de Nemours

Sales	$37 billion
Employees	110,000
Business	Diversified Chemicals, Fibers, Polymers, and Petroleum (Conoco)
Case Focus	Agricultural Pesticide (Chapter V)

More important, they illustrate how environmental costs can influence a wide variety of business decisions. These findings provide a strong rationale for asking how well a firm's managerial accounting system is serving these needs.

S.C. Johnson Wax
Sales   (Private)
Employees   13,000
Business   Chemical Specialty Products for Home Care,
              Insect Control and Personal Care
Case Focus   Household Pesticide (Chapter VI)

Cascade Cabinet
Sales $14 million
Employees   200
Business   Specialty Cabinets
Case Focus   Company-wide (Chapter VII)

Eldec
Sales $140 million
Employees   1,100
Business   Electronic Instruments for Aerospace Industry
Case Focus   Company-wide (Chapter VII)

Heath Tecna Aerospace
Sales $100 million
Employees   1,000
Business   Components for aerospace industry
Case Focus   Company-wide (Chapter VII)

Spectrum Glass
Sales $12 million
Employees   160
Business   Specialty Sheet Glass (Chapter VII)

Green Ledgers is aimed at the many business executives and managers who are already conscious of environmental issues, but unsure about the answers to four basic questions: What are their environmental costs? How large are these costs? Where do they arise within

3

the organization? And how can they be better managed? In striving to answer these questions, companies will better equip themselves to reconcile environmental goals with sound business decisions—and to achieve greater "eco-efficiency." In addition, the findings from the case studies can help professional associations, regulatory agencies, educators, and future managers institutionalize better environmental accounting practices within the business community.

2. Competing Definitions

Environmental accounting is a young and evolving field still burdened by confusion over definitions. In this book, which concentrates on the management of internal environmental costs by business, accounting is taken to mean the systematic collection, organization, and communication of information on an organization's activities. Environmental accounting is an umbrella term that includes accounting at the national and company levels. More detailed explanations of various facets of environmental accounting are provided elsewhere (U.S. EPA, 1995; Business Roundtable, 1993).

For decades, environmental economists have recognized that traditional measures of national economic performance are biased toward the consumption of natural resources. Indeed, as noted in a previous WRI report, "a country could exhaust its mineral resources, cut down its forests, erode its soils, pollute its aquifers, and hunt its wildlife and fisheries to extinction" without recording this against its income (Repetto et al., 1989). Many nations are working to incorporate natural resource depreciation into national accounts (UNCTC, 1992). One goal is to revise estimates of the gross domestic product—basically, "greening the GDP."

At the company level, it is important to distinguish between the environmental costs borne by the firm versus those imposed on society as "social costs." *(See Figure 1.)* Health effects from breathing polluted air, the impact of water pollution on fisheries, or soil contamination are classic examples of social costs, or externalities. On the other hand, regulations, corporate policies, consumer preferences, and community pressures shift some social costs back to firms. Discharge limits, emissions taxes, product take-back requirements, and other policy instruments also create economic incentives for firms to reduce potential environmental impacts—to make the "polluter pay." Some of these costs are already being passed on to firms as expenses for pollution-control technology, environmental staff, and permitting fees. Nonetheless, because many of these costs are indirect, long-term, and contingent, they tend to go unrecognized.

Much of the current debate about corporate environmental accounting centers on "full cost accounting"—a phrase often misinterpreted. Within the accounting profession, full cost accounting means that all manufacturing, sales, and administrative costs are allocated to products. Recently, a number of environmental and business leaders have also used full cost accounting to describe the practice of introducing environmental costs once considered external into corporate decision-making. This broader interpretation encompasses the range of private and social costs imposed throughout a product's life cycle, from raw material extraction to product disposal.

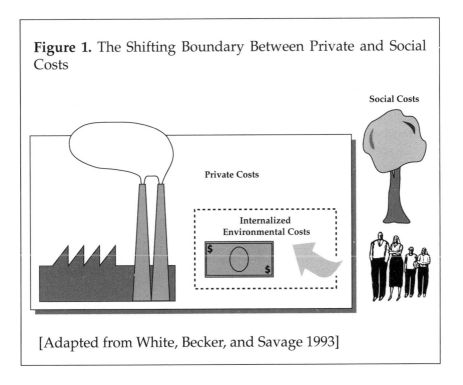

Figure 1. The Shifting Boundary Between Private and Social Costs

Social Costs

Private Costs

Internalized Environmental Costs

[Adapted from White, Becker, and Savage 1993]

This concept has also been extended to product pricing. In the words of Frank Popoff, President and CEO of Dow Chemical, "full cost accounting describes how goods and services can be priced to reflect their true environmental costs, including production, use, recycling and disposal" (Popoff and Buzzelli, 1993). Under such a system, consumers could evaluate the full economic consequences of their choices, both internal and external. If all firms followed suit, shelf prices might lead customers to buy goods with lower total costs. However, any firm that unilaterally raises the prices of its more polluting products will be at a disadvantage vis à vis lower priced competitors. For whatever reasons, this provocative notion has yet to be put into practice.

Unlike the broader conceptions of full cost accounting and pricing, the casework presented here avoids an explicit accounting of social costs. But within this narrower view lies ample opportunity for firms to improve how they account for and manage their internal environmental costs (De Andraca and McCready, 1994). Thus, the focus here is on environmental accounting within the company, especially on *managerial accounting*—the diverse and largely unregulated practices by which firms record, analyze, and utilize information for in-house purposes.

At an enterprise level, firms also prepare financial reports for external parties, principally investors, securities regulators, and tax authorities. This practice, referred to as *financial accounting*, is guided by explicit standards known in the United States as Generally Accepted Accounting Principles (or GAAP). To date, most corporate attention to environmental accounting has been concentrated on financial accounting, particularly on the enormous liabilities arising from the remediation of contaminated property (CICA, 1993). Estimates of such liabilities range from $500–$750 billion nationally (Adams, 1992). With past financial and environmental decisions still playing out, the challenge for business is to avoid even larger environmental costs from current and future actions.

3. Why Should Firms Account for Environmental Costs?
Firms account for environmental costs for the same reason they account for other costs—because they affect the bottom line. Spending on "pollution abatement and control" by U.S. manufacturers is

running at 0.9 percent of sales and rising, according to statistics collected by the U.S. Census Bureau (OTA, 1994). As shown in Figure 2, this steady increase prompts firms to get a better fix on the magnitudes and sources of environmental costs. While these total costs may seem minor, the environmental component is probably significantly understated.

In fact, pollution abatement and control represent only a portion of the overall cost of a firm's environmentally driven activities. Environmental costs associated with other activities can be much greater. A company's choice of raw materials, manufacturing

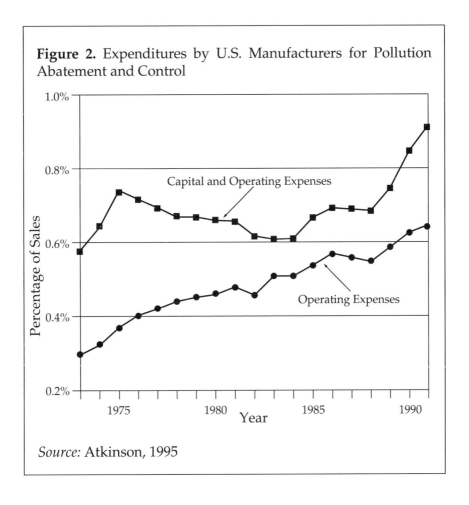

Figure 2. Expenditures by U.S. Manufacturers for Pollution Abatement and Control

Source: Atkinson, 1995

processes, and product design can profoundly affect these costs. Evidence presented in the WRI case studies shows that for certain products and facilities, environmental costs may account for 20 percent of total costs.

The size and upward trend in environmental costs is striking, but such aggregate information is of little use to individual firms struggling to control their own expenses. Managers need more details on these costs as they affect product, process, and site-level decisions inside the firm. Better information is needed on the impact of environmental factors on design, production, and marketing, as well as on conventional environmental "line items," such as waste management.

The push for better environmental accounting is on. Outside stakeholders are driving firms to account for environmental costs. Many corporations now volunteer estimates of their aggregate environmental spending in annual reports. The U.S. Securities and Exchange Commission (SEC) already requires businesses to follow certain procedures in recognizing and disclosing environmental liabilities in their financial reporting (U.S. SEC, 1993). The SEC is also pressing for even greater disclosure of environmental liabilities, especially the potential costs of cleaning up contaminated sites (Murphy, 1994; Roberts, 1994). A recent agreement between the SEC and the U.S. Environmental Protection Agency (EPA) promises a greater exchange of environmental and financial data.

A growing number of state and federal environmental regulations also call on firms to better account for environmental costs and benefits. Proposed EPA guidelines for hazardous waste generators ask firms to account for the "true costs" of waste management and to consider allocating them to the offending activities (U.S. EPA, 1993). Washington, New Jersey, and other states require firms to estimate environmental costs and to undertake some "materials accounting" in the course of mandatory pollution prevention planning. Although these represent external demands for environmental cost information, firms can put the information to good use in-house.

4. Shortcomings of Traditional Accounting

Before the advent of sophisticated management information systems, it would have been prohibitively expensive to operate multiple accounting systems to satisfy both external financial reporting obligations and internal managerial information needs. For more than 60 years, tax reporting and SEC disclosure requirements have shaped how most companies account for costs and how accountants and managers are trained. Unfortunately, the preoccupation with financial reporting requirements has been at the expense of developing accounting systems that can deliver managerial information for internal use.

Traditionally, most environmental costs within firms are not traced directly to their sources. Rather, they are accumulated in overhead pools and allocated across production processes in proportion to such simple measures as labor hours or units of output. As long as the costs stay small, sorting out the exact contributions of every process or activity scarcely seems worth the trouble. Indeed, many firms consider more accurate tracking analogous to charging employees for every paper clip—an overwhelming administrative expense for little or no benefit.

Yet, when the costs become significant, and when different parts of an organization contribute to them unequally, tighter accounting can more than pay for itself. Consider what happens when inaccurate cost allocations misrepresent costs, thus sending the wrong signals to managers and other decision-makers inside the company. In product costing, for example, this failure can skew the evaluation of profitability across a slate of products. Using traditional cost allocation methods, products with relatively lower environmental costs subsidize those with higher environmental costs (Kreuze and Newell, 1994).

With better internal accounting for environmental costs, product margins would not erode across the board. While some products would experience upward cost pressure, the cost of other "cleaner" products would fall. As a result, a better handle on environmental costs can influence which products a company decides to manufacture. While top management necessarily focuses on the bottom line of the income statement, countless individual decisions are made using more detailed, but imperfect, cost data.

Given the practical shortcomings of conventional accounting information, it is not surprising that managers develop a distorted picture of environmental costs. Consider the hypothetical manufacturing cost sheet presented in Figure 3. Familiar to managers in many industries, this product-oriented format itemizes the main elements of costs, both fixed and variable, to show the relative contributions of labor, capital, and material inputs. But a quick search of the sheet for "environmental costs" turns up only a single item, the charge for wastewater treatment, at 15 cents per pound of product, or less than 2 percent of the total manufacturing cost. In fact, this rather obvious environmental cost represents just the tip of the iceberg.

Of course, environmental costs are driven by many activities that vary in complexity among sites and over time (Hamner and Stinson, 1995). Consider a firm that uses a particular chemical in production. The accounting system already tracks the purchase of the material. But the costs associated with its use do not stop there. The costs of storing the chemical may be higher due to environmental considerations. The company may incur larger costs for treating contaminated rinse water or managing the resulting sludge. Securing the necessary permits, monitoring compliance, and subsequent reporting also represent real costs. Depending on the nature of the facility, use of this material might also force the company to pay for additional worker training.

The point is that decisions as common as choosing a process chemical can give rise to various environmental costs that can be difficult to recognize or quantify. A product designer, purchasing agent, or product manager might well select one chemical that appears less costly than another, but that entails higher overall costs for the firm. The situation is considerably more complicated for larger firms that manage hundreds of materials at multiple facilities. Most firms have only a rough idea of how much a specific product or process contributes to facility-wide environmental costs.

Ultimately, managers must look beyond their traditional sources of cost information to develop a truer picture of environmental costs. But even existing cost information, when examined through an environmental lens, yields new insights. Look again at the hypothetical cost sheet, as depicted in Figure 4. Environmental costs are hidden in many of the conventional cost categories. At least some portion of costs that are commonly scored as "labor" or "materials" are a consequence of environmental objectives.

Figure 3. A Typical Manufacturing Cost Statement

PRODUCT MANUFACTURING COST STATEMENT

Product: K004 (Standard Grade)
Production Volume: 9,958 pounds
Production Period: May 15, 1995–June 14, 1995

Variable Costs

Item	Factors	Usage	Cost	Unit Cost
Raw Materials	$2.27/lb	11,840	$26,877	$2.70/lb
Intermediates	$0.87/lb	2,443	$2,125	$0.21/lb
Additives	$11.32/lb	89	$1,007	$0.10/lb
Utilities	$0.04/kW-hr	10,000	$400	$0.04/lb
Direct Labor	$27.40/hour	520	$14,248	$1.43/lb
Packaging	$0.60/pkg.	312	$187	$0.02/lb
Wastewater Treatment	$0.01/gal	150,000	$1,500	$0.15/lb
Total Variable Cost			**$46,345**	**$4.65/lb**

Fixed Costs

Item	Cost
Supervisor	$5,600
Fixed Labor	$12,327
Depreciation	$2,377
Divisional Overhead	$4,300
General Services & Admin.	$5,412
Total Fixed Cost	**$30,016**

Total Variable Cost	$46,345
Total Fixed Cost	$30,016
Total Manufacturing Cost	$76,361
Unit Manufacturing Cost	$7.67 per pound

All these myriad costs imposed on firms for environmental reasons are economic signals. So too are budding consumer preferences for "greener" products and shareholder preferences for corporations that rein in environmental liabilities. Firms that fail to

11

Figure 4. Some Environmental Costs Hidden in a Typical Cost Statement

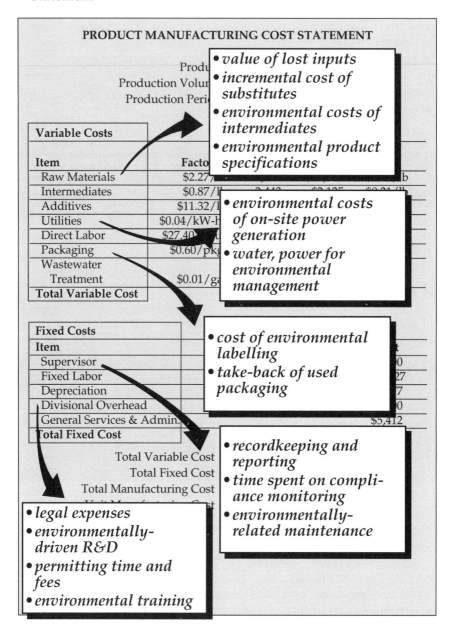

detect and respond to these signals will shoulder larger economic burdens that can only weaken their competitiveness.

The wiser course of action is to truly internalize environmental costs—not merely to bear them, but to anticipate and manage them. This means identifying the activities that give rise to them. Firms must be able to generate, evaluate, and implement alternatives to the status quo. They must be able to motivate executives, managers, and employees toward this common goal. In this endeavor, more effective, accurate accounting is crucial.

B. Magnitudes and Sources of Environmental Costs

1. The WRI Case Studies

In 1993, the World Resources Institute (WRI) began exploring how firms account for environmental costs. Working with three teams of academic investigators, WRI initiated nine case studies to improve understanding of environmental accounting through the participation of companies facing real business and environmental challenges.

The firms consulted include five major corporations: Amoco Oil, Ciba-Geigy, Dow Chemical, E.I. Du Pont de Nemours, and S.C. Johnson Wax. These diverse firms span several industries. Each has its own environmental challenges and corporate culture. In addition, one case study was undertaken of four mid-sized firms in Washington state—Cascade Cabinet, Eldec, Heath Tecna, and Spectrum Glass—that are obliged by state regulatory requirements to assess the costs and benefits of pollution prevention opportunities. Their experience expands the scope of this research, providing a look at some of the special problems faced by smaller firms.

Our purpose was not to pass judgment. Rather, we sought to ground this research in real-world practices, borrowing from the experience of those already employing some elements of environmental accounting. While the case studies are by no means a random sample, the findings apply to a broad cross-section of the business community. The studies are based on a review of economic and environmental information gathered through on-site interviews with corporate, divisional, and plant-level personnel. Most of the studies focus on particular products to illustrate the way many managerial accounting systems are organized. In all cases, participating firms reviewed the findings and screened confidential information.

Each firm was encouraged to focus on its internal costs, not on externalities. Otherwise, they were free to define costs as they chose. No single definition emerged, but most identified these costs as resources devoted to compulsory or voluntary actions to achieve environmental objectives. For example, capital costs for pollution control equipment are environmental costs, as are salaries of corporate environmental staff. Furthermore, the incremental cost of cleaner process technologies, extra processing steps, and less-polluting materials can be considered environmental. The failure to meet environmental goals also has costs, so regulatory fines, remediation costs, and even losses in sales were considered environmental costs.

The case study results presented are a rich store of business experience. While each of the cooperating firms has its own special characteristics, the collective findings afford fresh insight into the magnitudes and sources of environmental costs encountered by most firms. Section C examines several business applications of such information, and Section D builds on these results and work at WRI to offer practical guidance to firms ready to improve their environmental and economic performance through environmental accounting.

2. Aggregate Environmental Costs

Just how large are environmental costs? Corporate executives and other readers who want to go straight to the bottom line can turn to Table 2 for a glimpse of the gross magnitude of such costs uncovered at the five large firms. These numbers might satisfy initial curiosity about how large environmental costs can be. The double-digit percentages could well spur other firms to analyze their own environmental costs. But the magnitude of costs is not the whole story. The real value of environmental accounting lies behind these aggregate figures. By digging more deeply into the composition of the totals, the "behavior" of these costs, and other underlying factors, firms can link cost reduction to significant improvements in environmental performance. Since these costs refer only to the spe-

14

Table 2. Aggregate Environmental Costs from Selected Case Studies

Case Study	Finding
Amoco Oil	Nearly 22 percent of operating costs (excluding feedstock) were considered environmental at the Yorktown Refinery.
Ciba-Geigy	The environmental component was estimated at over 19 percent of manufacturing costs (excluding raw materials) for one chemical additive.
Dow Chemical	Between 3.2 and 3.8 percent of the manufacturing cost for a polymer-based product was considered environmental.
Du Pont	Over 19 percent of manufacturing cost was identified as environmental for one agricultural pesticide.
S.C. Johnson Wax	Environmental costs identified for one consumer product were approximately 2.4 percent of the net sales.

cific products, product lines, or facilities studied, they should not be extrapolated to the companies at large.

A quick glance at the figures in Table 2 could easily be misleading. Consider the S.C. Johnson and Dow cases. The numbers suggest that the relatively modest environmental cost percentages associated with these two products means that environmental issues are not that important. But a closer look at the S.C. Johnson case reveals that environmental costs exceed the operating profit for this product. In the case of Dow, the use of a seemingly inexpensive solvent was creating environmental challenges that jeopardized an

15

entire product line. On the other hand, estimated environmental costs may actually exaggerate the net economic impact on firms. Costs that are arguably environmental (e.g., equipment for closed-loop recycling or leak-detection programs) sometimes provide multiple benefits such as greater occupational safety or enhanced product quality. Furthermore, where environmental costs appear very large, a significant share of the total may consist of fixed expenses that have little net impact on cash flow. The important message is that no single number can adequately reflect the importance of environmental costs or their potential relevance to operational and strategic decision-making.

Furthermore, these estimates do not allow any meaningful comparisons of environmental costs across the case studies. A close inspection of Table 2 shows that each company has its own way of expressing aggregate environmental costs (e.g., as a percentage of product manufacturing costs, as a portion of operating costs, or as a share of net sales). Indeed, appropriate measures are industry-specific and often vary within a firm. In the petroleum industry, for instance, it makes sense to evaluate refinery operations exclusive of the changing cost of crude oil and other feedstocks. For a consumer products firm like S.C. Johnson—where distribution, marketing, and sales dominate product costs—net sales are a more meaningful gauge of the importance of environmental costs. In the Dow case, managers excluded the cost of operating labor devoted to environmental activities, arguing that attention to the environment is part of every employee's job. In the Amoco case, the portion of maintenance devoted to environmental activities was estimated and included in the total environmental cost number.

Clearly, there is no universal way to define environmental costs. Firms must tailor their own definitions to suit their intended uses—whether they be cost control, product pricing, capital budgeting, staff incentives, or other uses.

3. Breaking Out Environmental Costs

From a strategic perspective, firms must mind all costs. But in the short-term, managers generally focus on the most easily controlled costs. For these reasons, companies routinely distinguish between variable and fixed costs. Figure 5 shows the relative fixed and variable portions of environmental and non-environmental manufacturing costs of Du Pont's agricultural pesticide. Roughly four fifths of the environmental cost of the product are fixed, suggesting fewer opportunities to reduce environmental costs quickly.

The conventional accounting distinction between fixed and variable costs can lead to some confusion about the "controllability" of environmental costs. Over the long-run, all costs become variable. Many costs are recorded as "variable" or "fixed," depending on whether they vary with production volume. Off-site waste disposal is a classic example of a variable cost because it rises and falls with the quantity of production. But many types of environmental costs can vary with factors other than production. For

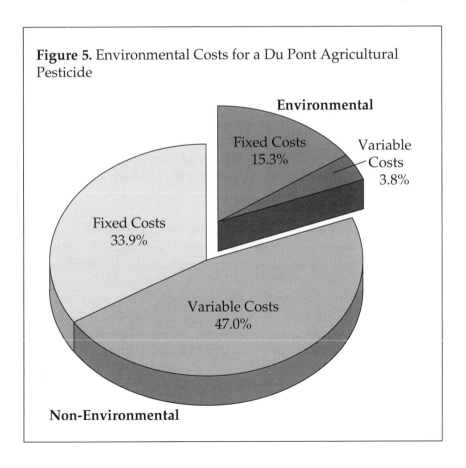

Figure 5. Environmental Costs for a Du Pont Agricultural Pesticide

Environmental

Fixed Costs
15.3%

Variable
Costs
3.8%

Fixed Costs
33.9%

Variable Costs
47.0%

Non-Environmental

example, those associated with emissions monitoring and reporting in a plant would change very little with the amount of product manufactured (ignoring the issue of regulatory thresholds), but could be lowered with a change of technology or materials.

What are the components of aggregate environmental cost within firms? As the breakdown of costs at Amoco's Yorktown refinery in Figure 6 illustrates, such costs show up in maintenance, administration, and stipulations on product quality (e.g., volatility limits on gasoline). The more obvious costs of waste treatment and disposal, though significant, are dwarfed by the sum of environmental costs extracted from cost categories that are not exclusively environmental.

Other cases exhibit similarly diffuse environmental costs. For the consumer product at S.C. Johnson, the direct environmental costs of manufacturing totalled less than 0.3 percent of the manufacturing cost. But the environmental costs in marketing, research and development, and product registration proved significant.

As the cases reveal, many environmental activities are simply not tracked and recorded as "environmental." One example is the time spent by operating personnel on environmental training, monitoring, and compliance. The Ciba-Geigy, Dow, and S.C. Johnson case studies speak to the difficulty of quantifying the environmental component of such ostensibly non-environmental accounts.

4. Organizational Dimensions of Environmental Costs

The case studies contain many examples of environmental costs that are allocated across departments and products, blurring the links between costs and their underlying drivers. As just one example, the time and resources that corporate environmental professionals at S.C. Johnson devote to issues arising from the use of solvents in certain products is allocated across all products on the basis of sales dollars instead of traced to specific products. Similar allocation practices were observed in all of the cases.

The organizational schematic in Figure 7 suggests just a few of the numerous places within a corporation where environmental costs can arise. In larger, more complex corporations, decisions made in one part of the organization frequently create environ-

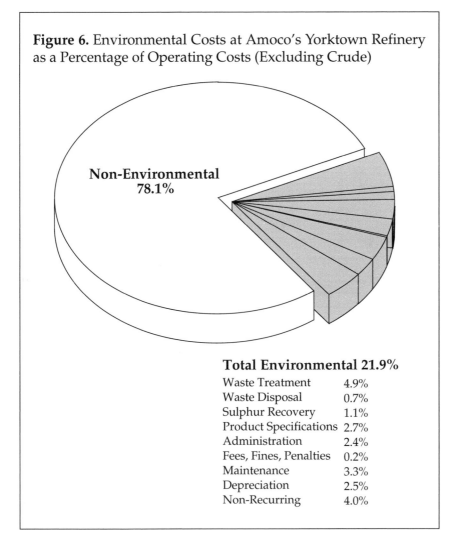

Figure 6. Environmental Costs at Amoco's Yorktown Refinery as a Percentage of Operating Costs (Excluding Crude)

Non-Environmental 78.1%

Total Environmental 21.9%

Waste Treatment	4.9%
Waste Disposal	0.7%
Sulphur Recovery	1.1%
Product Specifications	2.7%
Administration	2.4%
Fees, Fines, Penalties	0.2%
Maintenance	3.3%
Depreciation	2.5%
Non-Recurring	4.0%

mental costs elsewhere in the company. The corporate hierarchy of divisions, business units, and plants imposes cascading overheads on managers. The resulting disconnection between those who contribute to environmental costs and those ultimately held accountable hinders environmental management, even in smaller, less complex organizations. The practical challenge for accounting sys-

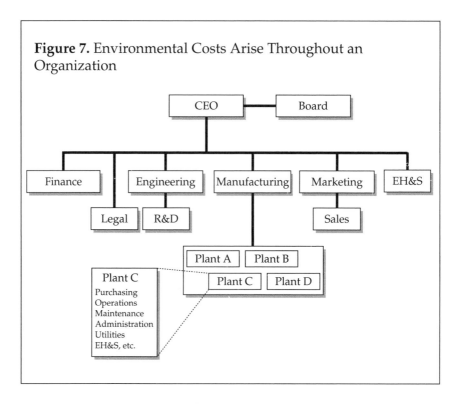

Figure 7. Environmental Costs Arise Throughout an Organization

tems is to hold decision-makers responsible for their actions, regardless of where in the corporation the consequences materialize.

What difference does it make if maintenance on environmental equipment is tallied as an "environmental" rather than "maintenance" expenditure? In one sense, none. As firms assess their overall performance, whether a particular expense item carries a green flag in the accounting system is secondary to responsible management. Yet, tracing costs back to specific decisions helps managers better understand cause and effect. Decisions about which products to manufacture and what technology to employ can increase or ease the environmental management burden on the firm. But if those costs show up only in the general maintenance budget, managers will systematically underestimate the benefits of cleaner production. This commingling of environmental costs in non-environmental accounts, combined with the gaps between costs and the activities that give rise to them, conceal the true magnitude of environmental costs. No wonder managers find it difficult to appreciate the full impact of environmental concerns on their business.

The case studies also demonstrate that firms can overcome these obstacles and better manage environmental costs. Specifically, the managerial accounting system can help decision-makers coordinate environmental activities and other activities within inherently complex organizations. The system can be used to monitor relevant environmental cost information and to communicate environmental objectives through charges and rewards to motivate employees.

Many managers may consider the practice of rolling environmental expenses into overhead accounts as a practical necessity and fear that implementing a more rigorous accounting for environmental costs would be prohibitively expensive. They might be right, but the answer depends on whether better accounting for environmental costs will lead to more sound decisions, and, ultimately, a more competitive company. To answer this question requires an even more detailed look at how such information can be put to use.

C. Business Uses of Environmental Cost Information

Environmental accounting is more than "green bean counting." However interesting the numbers, firms will not go through the trouble and expense of developing them unless they can be used to enhance productivity and profitability. Drawing on examples from the case studies, this section demonstrates several of the many ways in which information on environmental costs can influence business decision-making. In traditional business uses, environmental costs figure in the selection of product mix, the evaluation of alternative manufacturing inputs, the comparison of costs across facilities, and product pricing. Also explored here are the ways that better cost information supports more cost-effective environmental management, whether in evaluating waste management options, prioritizing environmental initiatives, or assessing opportunities for pollution prevention. Although these examples reflect private sector experience, the uses have broad applicability in public sector

21

decision-making, as acknowledged in the National Performance Review (Gore, 1993). Other uses of environmental cost information, including the capital budgeting process and product design, have been described elsewhere (White et al., 1993; Fiskel and Wapman, 1994; GEMI, 1994; Savage and White, 1994).

1. Product Mix Decisions

In choosing what to produce, all manufacturers must carefully weigh customer demand, capacity constraints, product profitability, and other factors. Yet, because measures of profitability depend on projected revenues and projected costs, and because environmental costs are so frequently misallocated, products with relatively higher environmental costs are often subsidized by those with lower ones. With only this distorted picture of profitability to work with, firms undervalue the direct economic benefits of products with lower environmental costs.

To illustrate, the principal environmental issue facing Spectrum Glass springs from the use of cadmium oxide, a colorant for which no adequate substitutes are available. Cadmium oxide is used in just one product line—"ruby red" glass. Although the manufacture of ruby red produces more hazardous waste than that of other glasses, the resulting environmental costs are allocated across all products. At present, making ruby red glass appears profitable. But if pending regulations on the release of cadmium take effect, costs will rise so sharply that the firm will drop the product from their portfolio. In this case, the prospective hike in environmental costs is easily attributable to the product responsible.

This is not always the case. The Amoco case study provides an especially rich illustration of how hard it can be to trace environmental costs to products. Petroleum refining is a highly integrated manufacturing process that provides a spectrum of hydrocarbon products. Any process change can affect the yield of all of the products. At Amoco, the product mix is determined above the refinery level, based on such factors as regional and seasonal demand and product margins. Once the product mix has been selected, the refinery uses a computer model to translate production targets into operating parameters for the individual units. This model helps management meet production objectives at lowest cost. As a practical matter, the model ignores all costs that are expected to remain fixed, including many environmental costs. But since some of the components of environmental costs do change with product mix, omitting them could bias the results toward mixes with relatively higher environmental costs. Conversely, incorporating variable environmental costs into decisions on product mix and refinery-operating parameters can lower overall costs. (Whether this effect is small or large could not be determined during the course of the case study.) To be sure, few industries are forced to contend with the extreme process complexity found in petroleum refining, but those that do should examine the implications of a changing product mix on environmental costs.

2. Choosing Manufacturing Inputs

The choice of which materials to use in a manufacturing process often depends on cost as well as safety, reliability, performance, and other criteria. Consider a hypothetical choice between two chemical substitutes. The cheaper material triggers additional compliance costs, such as those for permit preparation, fees, monitoring, and disposal. In contrast, using the more expensive material entails lower environmental costs. The additional environmental costs of the less expensive material may not be fully appreciated by the purchasing department, and production managers may be charged for only part of these higher costs. For this reason, understanding how environmental costs depend on the choice of materials can lead to more informed selection of raw materials, intermediates, and other process inputs.

At Cascade Cabinet, a decision to switch from nitrocellulose lacquer to a slightly more expensive conversion varnish saved the company significant sums. The lacquer, a hazardous material and source of volatile organic chemicals (VOCs), had been used to coat cabinet components. Residual dust from the lacquer, touched off by a welding spark, caused a serious fire and one million dollars in damage. Substituting the conversion varnish not only reduced the risk of another explosion, it also lowered the cost of insurance, waste disposal, and air permit fees. Fueled by these tangible savings, Cascade has asked one of its suppliers to develop a high-quality, water-based stain to replace another solvent-based product now in use.

23

Although Cascade Cabinet is a relatively small firm, the idea that different process inputs can lower environmental costs is also valid for larger companies. For example, the world market for crude oil offers various grades, each containing different types and amounts of impurities. Removing these impurities carries environmental costs at the various stages of refining. Amoco is currently exploring how the choice of crude oil influences environmental costs. By developing a better understanding of how environmental costs vary with different varieties of crude, the company can select those whose use lowers overall costs. This demonstrates how important the general link between process inputs and environmental costs is to the search for more cost-effective substitutes.

3. Assessing Pollution Prevention Projects
Over the past three decades, efforts to limit industrial pollution have focused largely on end-of-pipe pollution control. More recently, the emphasis has moved upstream, toward process-oriented preventive solutions that reduce the amount of pollutants generated. Unfortunately, under typical management accounting practices, many costs avoided by such changes are not credited to the successful manager, so pollution prevention projects often compete on an unequal footing with projects reliant on the existing pollution control and waste disposal infrastructure. A study of 29 chemical plants found that source reduction activities were most likely where some sort of environmental accounting was being practiced (Dorfman et al., 1992). Motivated by similar discoveries, others are providing tools and training to aid business in this effort (NEWMOA, 1994).

Recognizing the importance of this information, the Washington State pollution prevention planning rules require firms to scrutinize their operations and costs (Washington DOE, 1992). (See Chapter VII.) Through this planning process, Eldec, an electronics manufacturer that sells to the military and civilian aerospace industry, discovered that its generation of hazardous waste, and the corresponding costs, were driven by the frequency of preventative maintenance and cleaning. By making minor procedural changes that didn't reduce product quality, reliability or production, Eldec cut its use of hazardous cleaning solvents, its maintenance costs, and its hazardous waste generation.

Also searching for ways to reduce hazardous wastes, Cascade Cabinet managed to save $100,000 annually on wood scrap. This unused material is now chipped and sold to a particle-board manufacturer, and sales bring in three times the disposal cost. The investment in a large grinder plus one additional hour of work each morning was offset by direct savings within just one year.

The firms studied in Washington State had taken steps to prevent pollution before the planning requirements were introduced. But even though the pollution prevention legislation cannot be credited for all of the newly uncovered opportunities, all four firms contend that preparing the required plans had been worthwhile. This finding is being corroborated in New Jersey, where similar, but even more demanding planning requirements apply (N.J. DEP, 1995). In particular, more precisely quantifying environmental savings justified some projects that might otherwise have been rejected and strengthened the hand of in-house pollution prevention advocates. Washington State Department of Ecology publications document many examples of firms besides Eldec and Cascade that have undertaken pollution prevention projects as a consequence of the planning process (Washington DOE, 1993).

4. Evaluating Waste Management Options
Firms must routinely choose among various waste management methods. Because of persistent pressures to reduce operating expenses, costs naturally figure into these decisions. However, the case studies reveal that quantifying the true costs of managing wastes or the potential savings from cleaner production is rarely simple.

The Du Pont case study demonstrates how a better understanding of environmental costs can make waste management more cost-effective. One of Du Pont's large wastewater streams has traditionally been managed by deep-well injection. As Figure 8 shows, if managers are charged the full absorption cost (both variable and fixed costs), deep-well injection—at 0.09 cents per pound—appears less costly than the alternatives. But look again. Much of the cost for deep-well injection is for pumping, while most of the cost for bio-treatment is fixed and does not change regardless of how wastes are managed. Once Du Pont analyzed costs, it

25

concluded that a switch to bio-treatment would save 0.04 cents per pound in out-of-pocket expenditures. While the facility has not yet phased out deep-well injection altogether, management now gives preference to biological treatment.

At Amoco's Yorktown Refinery, management decided several years ago to treat wastewater sludge and other wastes in a process unit called the coker. In a coker, residual fuel oils and heavy petroleum intermediates are thermally "cracked" to produce solid coke and such higher-value products as gasoline. When the original decision was made, little information was available on the cost of coking

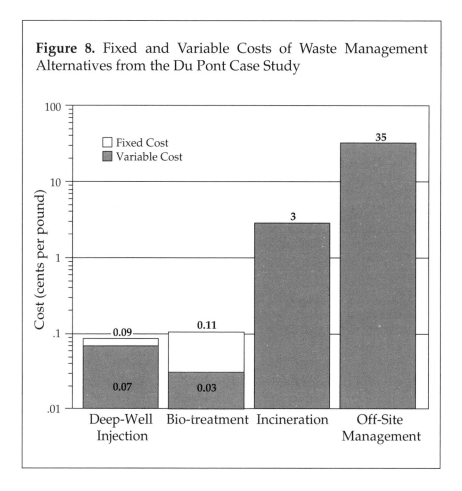

Figure 8. Fixed and Variable Costs of Waste Management Alternatives from the Du Pont Case Study

wastes, though the benefits of avoided costs for off-site sludge disposal were apparent. Later, a more detailed analysis revealed significant cost implications. Some had been anticipated, such as a slight reduction in the yield of higher-value products. Others, including higher maintenance costs, were not. Of course, even the best accounting information could not have predicted these unexpected costs. Yet, by tracking them after the decision had been implemented, Amoco could respond effectively. In retrospect, the company still backs the original decision, but its deepening understanding of the economics helps it to better manage the costs of waste coking and to respond more quickly to changing circumstances.

5. Comparing Environmental Costs Across Facilities
Environmental cost information can be influential as management compares operations within a firm. For example, firms can use such information to compare environmental performance across facilities and identify the best performers. The Ciba-Geigy case considered how environmental costs might be used in deciding where specific products should be manufactured. Many fixed costs of shared environmental facilities, such as existing incinerators and wastewater treatment plants, continue regardless of where the product is manufactured. The study identifies a subset of costs that would change if the product were shifted from one of the company's facilities to another. Internationally especially, these costs vary with both environmental regulations and such internal factors as the availability of trained personnel and waste management capacity.

Similarly, the case study based on a single Amoco refinery suggests how looking closer at environmental costs can influence the allocation of production among multiple refineries. For example, an earlier investment in technology for refining high-sulfur crudes permits the Yorktown Refinery to meet new regulatory requirements for low-sulfur diesel fuel. Even though this investment raises the facility's cost burden incrementally, the refinery now has a comparative cost advantage in meeting the new product requirement.

Environmental cost information readily lends itself to the development of internal benchmarks of comparative environmental performance. For instance, a computer chip manufacturer might want to determine the environmental cost per chip across its manufacturing sites or along the production chain. The Du Pont case study describes how the company prioritized more than 700 projects to reduce emissions by estimating the cost per pound of emissions eliminated. With so many options, this cost-effectiveness measure helped managers choose among the vast array of options. Du Pont developed a methodology for rank-ordering projects that considered cost/benefit ratios, regulatory requirements, and competitive factors. These projects each carry a "technology indicator" that permits Du Pont to leverage solutions across the corporation. Regulations still force some relatively costly expenditures, and project scheduling and other considerations can also influence the decision of which projects to undertake. Still, this scheme provides a consistent and formal way to evaluate trade-offs among competing proposals.

6. Pricing Products

From the "polluter pays" perspective, it makes sense to include all attendant environmental costs in a product's price. If an entire industry adopted this approach uniformly, customers could make more informed decisions on what products to purchase. While this notion is at present far from reality, a better understanding of private environmental costs did affect product pricing in at least one of the case studies.

Dow Chemical faced new, tougher limits under the 1990 Clean Air Act Amendments in addition to their corporate commitment to EPA's 33/50 Program, a voluntary campaign to lower emissions of seventeen toxic chemicals. These twin obligations implied significant new environmental costs in the manufacture of a polymer-based coating material and a large emitter of VOCs at the site. The company faced a stark choice: invest in pollution control or shut down the operation. Dow weighed the costs of additional investment against those of discontinuing operations. They also met with their industrial customers to explain that making the investment would assure a reliable continuing supply, but at higher cost. Thus, environmental cost information generated for internal decision-making purposes also helped justify the potential price increase. The new information convinced customers that Dow was making a genuine investment in the product's long-term viability, so in essence, they accepted a price premium.

D. A Practical Guide for Getting Started

1. Purpose

This guide is intended to help companies take steps toward better environmental accounting. The idea is to help business leaders—senior corporate executives as well as managers of plants and strategic business units—understand and manage environmental costs, while improving their overall decision-making. Despite the differences in firms' scope and scale, managers in smaller companies can adapt these concepts to their businesses. Similarly, these lessons from the private sector can serve non-profit and public sector organizations facing significant environmental challenges.

Trying environmental accounting does not entail a complete overhaul of current accounting and information systems. Even modest incremental changes in how data are collected, conveyed, and analyzed can yield important environmental and economic benefits. Moreover, as the case studies confirm, a well-designed and executed environmental accounting pilot project can uncover significant opportunities for improvement and suggest broader changes in company policy and practice.

There is no single recipe for getting started. The strategic objectives of the firm, the complexity of its environmental challenges, and its size and corporate culture together dictate the right approach. Even so, the case studies presented in the following chapters offer general lessons about how to assess and manage environmental costs. More specifically, this guide outlines how firms might adapt environmental accounting to their own needs and capabilities and proposes mechanisms for integrating environmental costs into business decision-making.

Companies can have more than one reason for undertaking environmental accounting. An informal survey of some two dozen corporate environmental professionals listed general managerial control as the most common reason for monitoring environmental capital and operating costs (Nagle, 1994). But respondents also cited other objectives, such as responding to investor interest, tracking the impact of government regulations, orienting waste minimization efforts, reporting to the public, and better understanding costs. This multiplicity of uses bolsters the case study findings.

Firms seeking a keener appreciation of their environmental costs may find some managers resistant. In part, their skepticism reflects a mistaken belief that environmental costs are already well known. At the outset of the case studies, a number of individuals indicated that they already knew where most environmental costs originate. But, more often than not, they were seeing only part of a much larger, more complicated picture. If the focus on sources and magnitudes of costs is limited, opportunities for improving environmental and economic performance will be missed.

Viewing environmental expenditures as an inevitable cost of doing business also impedes better management. Obviously, any company engaged in environmentally risky activities must take precautionary measures, and these actions will carry costs. But, to assume that these are inherent and inescapable forestalls the search for cleaner materials, technologies, and practices—a self-fulfilling prophecy and a self-limiting business outlook.

2. Conducting a Pilot Project

There is no reason to expect all firms to approach environmental accounting in the same way. But taken together, the case studies provide a picture of some basic elements in conducting a pilot project. These are:

Defining Boundaries
Anticipating Resources
Selecting Participants
Gathering Information
Evaluating Results

This section offers some direction for managers interested in applying environmental accounting to their own operations.

Defining Boundaries

In developing an environmental accounting pilot project, how broadly should the scope be defined? Is it practical to concentrate on an entire division? On a few product lines? On a single facility? The answer depends largely on the initial objectives. Some case study firms set out with clear objectives articulated at the corporate level for implementation throughout the organization. DuPont's corporate-wide objective of cost-effective waste reduction, for instance, cuts across its many business units and sites.

In other cases, external factors were the driving force for environmental accounting. The case studies of the Washington state firms demonstrate how mandatory pollution prevention planning can spur companies to re-evaluate environmental costs. In contrast, firms approaching environmental accounting voluntarily can start with a small number of processes, facilities, or product lines. Consider Amoco's focus on a single refinery or the product-oriented approach represented by the Ciba-Geigy, Dow, and S.C. Johnson cases. The key here is making the pilot project somehow representative of other company activities, so that the findings can be extended to the company as a whole.

Anticipating Resources
How much time and effort will the pilot project take? No company should expect to unravel its environmental costs all at once. As the case studies show, it takes time to sift through accounting data and to relate it to environmental and other business issues. A certain amount of detective work is required. So is time to understand how information flows through the firm, how this pattern influences behavior, and whether and how to implement change.

The resources necessary for the pilot project depend on the scope of the analysis and the complexity of the business. Realistically, a team of three to five people working part-time over three to four months can identify the most important aspects of environmental accounting for review. The team should be free to make this work a priority at regular intervals. For more extensive reviews in large and complex organizations, the practice of uncovering costs can be integrated into ongoing business processes. For example, over the last four years DuPont has incorporated a systematic search for costs into corporate environmental planning. There is no substitute for learning as you go.

As in any new initiative, senior management support is essential before embarking on a pilot project. Winning this commitment requires being clear about what can be accomplished and what is expected of participants. From a practical perspective, high-level commitment signals that the undertaking is worth the time and energy of others with valuable information and insights. This initial backing also assures that the project's recommendations will receive serious consideration.

Selecting Participants

Who should be involved in the process? Finding the right mix of talents and experience requires thinking not only about the pilot project, but also about the potential for sharing the findings within the organization. Even though the outcome of the pilot project cannot be foreseen, involving a cross-section of business functions and responsibilities will strengthen the effort and lend its conclusions greater credibility.

No single person, department, or level in the company commands all the information and knowledge needed to analyze environmental costs in detail. Indeed, a variety of individuals and departments must be engaged, preferably as a multidisciplinary team. This team could include members of senior management with profit and loss responsibility, corporate risk managers, managerial accountants, product managers, operating engineers, designers, environmental specialists, and others.

Involving individuals from outside the project's immediate focus can also be valuable. The case study companies worked in partnership with WRI and the academic investigators. In most cases, a senior manager responsible for environment, finance, or corporate planning catalyzed the company's efforts. But much of the information gathering was carried out by managers, accountants, engineers, and operators on-site at plants. The internal search for environmental costs can benefit from a fresh perspective on routine activities that those most deeply involved may overlook.

Critical to success is a dialogue across traditional boundaries. Sharing data and cross-fertilizing expertise are valuable in their own right. In addition, the pilot project affords the chance to jointly explore the environmental dimensions of production, R&D, marketing, and other compartmentalized functions. When Eldec began preparing its pollution prevention plan, the accounting department was leery of participating. Later, the company acknowledged the interaction between environmental and accounting personnel as an important benefit. Such crossover can be fostered in the context of other on-going activities. Involving managerial accountants in environmental compliance audits, for example, both acquaints accountants with general environmental issues and broadens the environmental staffs' view of business issues.

Gathering Information

Once the scope of the analysis is defined and the team assembled, the next step is to begin collecting information. Where should the project team begin? Considering the major environmental issues facing the product, process, or site is one way to start searching for environmental costs. For example, in both the Ciba-Geigy and Dow case studies, specific chemicals posed potentially significant environmental and occupational concerns, so a large portion of total environmental costs was driven by the handling, reclamation, recycling, or treatment of these materials. In the pilot project at Amoco's Yorktown refinery, interviewing managers about their perceptions of current and prospective environmental challenges helped steer the team to costs with environmental relevance.

The search for environmental costs is not just a paper exercise. Environmental accounting requires an understanding of the over-all business landscape, the company's core activities and capabilities, and the nature of environmental challenges. While this obviously involves an analysis of general ledgers, the accounting system is only one of many sources of information. Some others are listed in Table 3. Still more are sure to come to light during the pilot study, supplementing standard information in the accounting system and helping the team estimate costs not currently recorded.

This process of gathering information is inherently open-ended and iterative, as the decisions on waste coking at the Yorktown Refinery show. *(See Section C.4.)* In that case, the company's understanding of costs evolved gradually over time. As Figure 9 shows, without a deliberate search it literally took years to appreciate all the cost ramifications, even without fully quantifying them. Whether inadvertent or intentional, this process of discovery is a prerequisite to understanding and managing costs.

As the pilot project progresses, the team will discover costs that are motivated as much by environmental improvement as by "yield enhancement" or other descriptors of improved productivity. A

Table 3. Sample Sources for Environmental Cost Information

Environmental Costs	Information Sources
Permitting Fees and Fines	Regulatory Documents Management Estimates
Maintaining Environmental Equipment	Maintenance Logs Service Contracts
Non-Product Output	Emissions Estimates Production Logs
Process Penalties/Shut-downs	Operating Records
Depreciation	Capital Asset Ledger
Monitoring	Engineering Estimates Management Estimates
Environmental Auditing	Management Estimates
Training	Personnel, EHS Records Management Estimates

closed-loop solvent recycling system, while promising major environmental benefits, might be justified purely on the basis of reductions in solvent costs. How then is the company to score the associated costs? The adoption of more integrated, process-oriented investments for environmental protection makes answering this question more difficult. The U.S. Census Bureau is currently re-evaluating its guidance to firms on this point in the annual Survey of Pollution Abatement Costs and Expenditures (U.S. Department of Commerce, 1995). As the project team makes judgments on these issues, it must keep broader objectives in sight. Certainly, the case studies show that such difficulties do not pose significant obstacles, so long as assumptions are clearly identified and definitions uniformly applied.

Figure 9. Evolution of Cost Considerations in the Coking of Waste at Amoco's Yorktown Refinery

Costs	1987 Decision to Coke Waste	1991 Coker Upgrade	1993 Coker Upgrade
Capital	$	$	$
Operating	$	$	$
Coker Outages	–	$	$
Maintenance	✓	✓	$
Process Penalty	✓	✓	$
Permitting	✓	✓	✓
Product Certification	✓	✓	✓
Compliance, Record-keeping	–	✓	✓
Public, Govt. Relations	–	–	–
Fines, Penalties	–	–	–
Future Liability	–	–	–

Key: $ costs considered and quantified
　　✓ costs considered but not quantified
　　– costs judged insignificant or not recognized

Similar questions arise in the case of raw materials costs. Is the entire purchase cost "environmental?" Not if most raw materials are incorporated in products rather than discharged as waste. At one extreme, roughly 99 percent of the crude oil entering a refinery leaves as product. This 1-percent differential between inputs and products can still cost the company a great deal, but the entire cost of crude oil would be a gross overstatement of the environmental cost. In contrast, in some very low-yield manufacturing operations with large volumes of waste—in the Dow case, roughly five pounds for each pound of product—the value of materials destined to become waste might be a meaningful component of environmental costs.

Clearly, companies do not need to think about environmental costs to understand the basic importance of productivity. Simply defining such non-product output as an "environmental" cost will not change the basic drive to squeeze more product from a given amount of inputs. But recognizing these dual benefits can tip the balance in business decisions. This is the essence of Total Cost Assessment, a technique for incorporating pollution prevention benefits in capital budgeting and investment analysis (White et al., 1993; U.S. EPA, 1992). When Heath Tecna, a manufacturer of composite materials for the aerospace industry, applied this technique, it found that it was spending about $85,000 a year to dispose of hazardous wastes derived from materials that had cost nearly $5 million. Recognizing the disposal and materials savings helped convince Heath Tecna to invest in sophisticated technology for more efficient pattern layout and cutting.

Of course, even the best environmental cost information available will leave important gaps unfilled. For example, the case studies uncovered no direct evidence of accounting for the future environmental costs of current actions—an important concern of corporate risk managers and legal staff. Liabilities for current and future actions and intangible costs are extremely difficult to predict, let alone quantify. Where monetary estimates are possible, firms fear triggering financial disclosure requirements by coming up with a dollar figure. Although firms will find quantification difficult, these costs fall within the private cost domain (in Figure 1) and are integral to sound decision-making.

Future environmental liabilities also have positive counterparts. Unquantifiable environmental factors, including consumer perceptions of companies and products, can affect the bottom line through increased sales. These revenues could more than balance the readily quantified environmental components of labor, plant, and equipment. Success in preventing pollution, for example, can translate into improved community relations, greater worker satisfaction, lower public opposition to possible expansion, and even faster permit approval—all of which can reduce the firm's overall costs. Ignoring such intangible benefits, however hard to estimate, means making less than fully informed decisions.

Results of the Pilot Project

As these case studies demonstrate, the specific findings of the pilot project can be as varied as the businesses analyzed. Still, these preliminary results are likely to lead in three general directions. First, the scrutiny of environmental costs is likely to produce insights of direct relevance to the project itself. For example, identifying lower-cost waste management alternatives or more effective raw materials can prompt managers to alter practices. Second, the conclusions can highlight the need for change in company-wide environmental, accounting, or managerial practices. Discovering systemic biases in the allocation of environmental costs or gaps in accountability may require broad remedies. Finally, if the pilot study's findings are compelling, the company can extend its recommendations to other portions of the business or even to the whole firm. Although simply repeating the pilot project for every facility and product would be unnecessary, expanding the project's scope to cover groups of facilities or a division may uncover opportunities for higher level improvements in the accounting system.

In any event, to fully benefit from environmental accounting, companies must move from study to action. After reviewing the results of the pilot project, most firms will spot opportunities for improvement. Whether it is changing the flow of information, revising cost allocation schemes, or devising new incentives for encouraging more effective management, these changes are all driven by a single objective—integrating environmental considerations through better business decisions and management.

3. Managing Environmental Costs

There can be no universal prescription for how best to gather, evaluate, and act on environmental cost information. Still, from the exposure to the firms studied here, it is possible to distill five core recommendations for businesses:

- Inform decision-makers of the environmental costs they generate;
- Increase accountability of managers for environmental costs and benefits;
- Develop proxies that anticipate future costs and other measures of performance;
- Create incentives to address the causes of current and future costs; and

- Incorporate environmental accounting into ongoing business processes.

This final section outlines some practical implications of these overarching business needs.

Informing Decision-Makers

Information on environmental costs is meaningful only if it influences behavior. At a minimum, it must be communicated to the appropriate decision-makers. Regular summaries of environmental cost information can help key managers identify trends and promote greater awareness of where costs originate within the firm. This is not a question of providing more information, but more useful information.

As this project makes clear, many environmental costs are obscured by conventional accounting systems, so their magnitude and importance are underestimated. If their extent is communicated, the strategic significance of environmental management will be more apparent. Presenting aggregate cost numbers can be an effective way to direct attention to environmental issues. Yet, since costs can be managed only through the activities that create them, and since internal accounting systems typically order cost information by product, new ways of segmenting such costs may be required.

One alternative emerged in the S.C. Johnson case study. A number of the company's popular household products can be provided in aqueous (water-based) or organic solvent-based formulations. Consumers prefer the solvent-based formulations, which are faster-acting but no more effective than the aqueous alternative. For either formulation, the manufacturing costs are quite minor in relation to the total product cost. But the organic solvent in the pesticide product investigated contributes to local environmental issues at the manufacturing site, ultimately adding to environmental costs. Even small cost differentials can spell the difference between profit and loss for highly competitive products.

The S.C. Johnson case indicated that product profitability statements that segment costs by aqueous and solvent-based products could be useful. In the hypothetical example depicted in Figure 10, environmental costs, signified by the shaded coins, are essentially equal across Product Lines A, B, and C where aqueous and solvent-based products are grouped together. But when the products are separated by formulation, it becomes clear that solvent-based products can account for disproportionately greater environmental costs. Such analysis can stimulate consumer-education efforts on the efficacy and environmental merits of water-based products.

There are many other formats for examining environmental costs. One could compare environmental costs across manufacturing operations both within and between firms, as alluded to in Section C.5. Such analyses readily lend themselves to benchmarking and identifying best-of-class performance. Companies may discover other dimensions along which to disaggregate existing data.

Making Managers Accountable

While information on environmental costs is a powerful tool for decision-makers, it does not assure accountability. Assigning costs to the managers who control them is the objective of most firms. Unfortunately, bundled overheads that are opaque to managers and insensitive to their actions make doing so difficult. So why try? Because the company's objective is not just to cut expenses, but also to manage the activities that create them, and cost information provides a mechanism to connect responsible parties with environmental impacts.

Some managers may suspect that more accurately tracing costs to responsible products and processes will work to their disadvantage. No managers welcome significant increases in the costs they are paid to control, especially if the renegotiation of allocation schemes directly affects their performance and their pay. Indeed, any change in accounting practices creates internal winners and losers. But the conspicuous complaints of some must simply be weighed against the overall benefits to the firm of more rigorously assigning costs. Addressing transitional difficulties, including the timing of change and the reward systems for making good use of new information, should be a part of any recommended changes in the accounting system.

Many firms levy internal charges for use of on-site environmental facilities (e.g., for wastewater treatment, incineration, disposal) to bring the "polluter pays" principle inside the plant gate. Besides charging direct operating costs to specific process or prod-

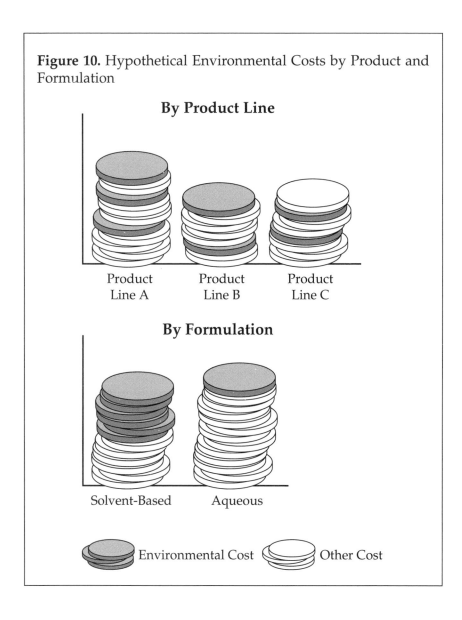

Figure 10. Hypothetical Environmental Costs by Product and Formulation

By Product Line

Product Line A   Product Line B   Product Line C

By Formulation

Solvent-Based   Aqueous

Environmental Cost   Other Cost

uct lines, firms can charge on a "cost-plus" basis to lower waste generation even further. Recently, Dow has considered increasing internal rates above the estimated operating and maintenance costs to match off-site commercial rates (Kirschner, 1994).

The practice of charging full costs or surcharges for waste management can have short-term consequences. For example, if on-site or off-site treatment costs were raised, managers might make changes in materials or operations that create higher out-of-pocket costs. In the extreme, a firm might discontinue products that are still profitable, but which appear too costly. But despite this potential pitfall, such charges can also signal companies to move toward cleaner and greener processes and products over the long run.

Managerial Incentives and Environmental Performance
Companies routinely evaluate managers' ability to meet specific objectives within budget. If predetermined business goals are met, annual bonuses and other rewards may follow. While this approach might be applied to environmental cost targets, inappropriate measures can encourage self-defeating or myopic behavior. For example, a heavy emphasis on reducing aggregate environmental costs could reward managers who cut back on environmentally related maintenance or R&D—activities essential to long-term environmental management.

An alternative is to connect incentives to the underlying activities that give rise to environmental costs. Such programs have been used for decades to drive progress on targets for productivity, safety, and quality. Amoco's gain-sharing plan, for instance, rewards employees for various measures of facility performance. The Yorktown refinery's waste-generation metric for the gain-sharing program excludes remediation costs associated with past contamination so that the current workforce is not penalized for decisions over which they had no control.

Including environmental metrics when managers are evaluated can rivet their attention and provide an incentive for reducing costs. Incentives schemes must also reflect the company's technological, economic, and organizational realities. Recognizing the inherently integrated character of petroleum refining, Amoco based its waste metric on the facility's overall performance. Tying the metric to waste generation at the process level instead might have invited suboptimal behavior. Specifically, penalizing the tank farm managers for the solid residues that settle out during storage would reward them for passing these impurities on to downstream process units. True, waste generation by the tank-farm would appear to fall, but downstream operating and maintenance problems and overall costs could significantly increase.

Identifying Proxies for Environmental Costs

A common theme that permeates the case studies is that future environmental costs, though inherently uncertain, are inevitable. Laws change, regulatory requirements evolve and expand. Actions that are perfectly legal today can create financial liabilities tomorrow. The challenge for managers is to avoid incurring future costs as they meet present demands.

One thing is clear: simply tracking historical costs is not good enough—it is blind to future changes in the rules of the game. Supplementing cost accounting with other indicators of environmental performance can help identify potential vulnerabilities before they become major cost factors. At Dow, a key solvent used in the manufacture of a polymer-based coating material represented only 1 percent of manufacturing costs, but release of this volatile organic air pollutant threatened to force the company to abandon an established product line. While the cost appeared modest, a changing regulatory climate and corporate commitments made use of this material increasingly costly. Attention was drawn to this challenge by tracking pounds of material rather than dollars.

Materials accounting—the systematic assessment of inputs, use, and release—for particular environmentally significant chemicals offers a proxy for potential future environmental costs. Reducing the release of chemicals into the environment may reduce future liabilities (all other things equal). That said, since the environmental impacts of chemicals vary widely, lowering total emissions does not necessarily reduce environmental consequences or liability exposure. Weighing the quantitative releases on the basis of existing scientific or regulatory estimates is a more meaningful way to compare potential future impacts. As one example, a kind of toxicity-weighted pollution unit can be calculated using available environmental standards and toxicological information (Grimstead et al., 1994). However imprecise, such approaches enable managers to develop cost-effective ways to reduce environmental risks. An added advantage is that this method does not require monetary estimates of future liabilities, so some significant legal issues are avoided (ELI, 1993). There is a great need for more work on practical indicators of environmental performance—to improve internal management as well as to report progress to outside stakeholders.

Integrating Environmental Accounting into Business Processes
Identifying, understanding, and managing environmental costs can be time-consuming and labor-intensive (Walley and Whitehead, 1994). Yet, this task is too important to be relegated to a one-time exercise. Rather than introducing another layer of internal reporting requirements or creating new accounting responsibilities for environmental units, firms should take advantage of their existing business processes.

Strategic planning offers a particularly promising opportunity for bringing environmental issues to bear on key company decisions. Corporate-wide environmental planning efforts, such as Du Pont's Corporate Environmental Plan, won't work without a realistic picture of the sources and magnitudes of environmental costs. Many other routine activities, such as capital budgeting and new product development, can be strengthened by explicitly incorporating environmental cost information. Firms undergoing major reorganization or "re-engineering" can introduce some elements of environmental accounting. Both the internal auditing of management systems and environmental auditing can help firms gather better environmental cost information and field better practices.

Incorporating environmental accounting into these processes offers two practical advantages over stand-alone environmental accounting efforts. For one, expertise and information essential to environmental accounting can be tapped or acquired at little additional cost. More important, linking environmental accounting to these other business processes helps infuse environmental thinking into core decision-making.

As a business tool, environmental accounting can soften the economic impact of environmental compliance. It can help management better understand what gives rise to costs and how they can be managed. It can also help managers assess the business and environmental implications of different alternatives. Environmental accounting can track crucial indicators over time, using information that is routinely recorded but rarely exploited, thus enhancing a firm's self-knowledge and its environmental accountability.

As firms come to terms with current environmental costs, they will appreciate that the boundary between private and social costs is porous and moving. Other environmental costs, now borne by society, will exert a growing influence over the decisions made within companies. The emerging shift toward greater self-regulation, market-based mechanisms, and green consumerism will inevitably drive companies to further internalize environmental externalities. Firms must begin to anticipate these broader environmental consequences and bring them to bear as they design new products, develop new technology, and make investments for the future.

REFERENCES

Adams, Jane. "Liability and the Financial Statement," *Directors and Boards,* Summer 1992.

Atkinson, Robert. Office of Technology Assessment, U.S. Congress: Washington, D.C. Personal communication, 1995.

The Business Roundtable. *Environmental Cost Accounting: Key Definitions and Terms.* Unpublished paper, November 10, 1993.

Canadian Institute of Chartered Accountants. *Environmental Costs and Liabilities: Accounting and Financial Reporting Issues.* Toronto, Canada: 1993.

De Andraca, Roberto and Ken McCready. *Internalizing Environmental Costs to Promote Eco-Efficiency.* Geneva: Business Council for Sustainable Development, 1994.

Dorfman, Mark, Warren Muir, and Catherine Miller. *Environmental Dividends: Cutting More Chemical Wastes.* New York, N.Y.: Inform, 1992.

Environmental Law Institute. *A Framework for Understanding the Relationship Between Environmental Liability and Managerial Decisions Affecting Pollution Prevention.* Prepared for the U.S. Environmental Protection Agency, September 1993.

Fiksel, Joseph and Kenneth Wapman. "How to Design for Environment and Minimize Life Cycle Cost," Mountain View, Calif.: Decision Focus Inc., 1994.

Global Environmental Management Initiative. *Finding Cost-Effective Pollution Prevention Initiatives: Incorporating Environmental*

Costs into Business Decision Making. A Primer. Washington, D.C.: September 1994.

Gore, Albert. *Reinventing Environmental Management.* Accompanying Report of the National Performance Review, Washington, D.C.: Office of the Vice President, September 1993.

Grimsted, Bradley, et al. "A Multimedia Assessment Scheme to Evaluate Chemical Effects on the Environment and Human Health," *Pollution Prevention Review,* Summer 1994, 259–268.

Hamner, Burt and Christopher Stinson, "Managerial Accounting and Environmental Compliance Costs," *Journal of Cost Management,* (forthcoming 1995).

Kirschner, Elizabeth. "Full Cost Accounting for the Environment: Gold Mine or Minefield?," *Chemical Week,* March 9, 1994, 25–26.

Kreuze, Jerry and Gale Newell. "ABC and Life-Cycle Costing for Environmental Expenditures," *Management Accounting,* February 1994, 38–42.

Murphy, Margaret. "Warning: Disclose Environmental Cost," *The New York Times,* September 4, 1994.

Nagle, George. "Business Environmental Cost Accounting Survey," presented at the Conference on Environmental Management in a Global Economy, Arlington, Virginia, 1994, 243–248.

New Jersey Department of Environmental Protection. *Early Findings of the Pollution Prevention Program, Part I.* Trenton, N.J.: NJDEP, 1995.

Northeast Waste Management Officials Association (NEWMOA). *Improving Your Competitive Position: Strategic and Financial Assessment of Pollution Prevention Projects.* Boston, MA: NEWMOA, 1994.

Office of Technology Assessment, U.S. Congress, *Industry, Technology and the Environment: Competitive Challenges and Business Opportunities,* Washington, D.C.: U.S. Government Printing Office, January 1994.

Popoff, Frank and David Buzzelli. "Full-Cost Accounting," *Chemical and Engineering News,* January 11, 1993, vol. 71, no. 2: 8–10.

Repetto, Robert, et al. *Wasting Assets: Natural Resources in the National Income Accounts.* Washington, D.C.: World Resources Institute, 1989.

Roberts, Richard. "Environmental Reporting and Public Accountability," presented to the Environmental Law Institute Corporate Management Workshop, Washington, D.C., June 6, 1994.

Savage, Deborah and Allen White, "New Applications of Total Cost Assessment: Exploring the P2-Production Interface," *Pollution Prevention Review,* Winter 1994–95, 7–15.

United Nations Centre on Transnational Corporations. *International Accounting and Reporting Issues: 1991 Review.* New York: United Nations, 1992.

U.S. Department of Commerce, Economics and Statistics Administration, Bureau of the Census, *Survey of Pollution Abatement Costs and Expenditures,* MA200, Washington, D.C.: U.S. Government Printing Office, 1995.

U.S. Environmental Protection Agency. *Total Cost Assessment: Accelerating Industrial Pollution Prevention Through Innovative Project Financial Analysis.* Prepared by Tellus Institute. Washington, D.C.: Office of Pollution Prevention and Toxics, U.S. Environmental Protection Agency, 1992.

___. *Guidance to Hazardous Waste Generators on the Elements of a Waste Minimization Program.* 58 FR 31114, Washington, D.C.: U.S. Environmental Protection Agency, May 28, 1993.

___. *An Introduction to Environmental Accounting as a Business Management Tool: Key Concepts and Terms.* Washington, D.C.: Office of Pollution Prevention and Toxics, U.S. Environmental Protection Agency, 1995.

U.S. Securities and Exchange Commission, Staff Accounting Bulletin Number 92, Washington D.C.: 1993.

Walley, Noah and Bradley Whitehead. "It's Not Easy Being Green," *Harvard Business Review.* May–June 1994, 46–52. (Also, follow-up letters: "The Challenge of Going Green," *Harvard Business Review,* July–August 1994, 37–50.)

Washington State Department of Ecology. *Economic Analysis for Pollution Prevention.* Bellevue: Department of Ecology Guidance Paper, 1992.

___. *Pollution Prevention Planning in Washington State Businesses.* Olympia, WA: May 1993.

White, Allen, Monica Becker, and Deborah Savage, "Environmentally Smart Accounting: Using Total Cost Assessment to Advance Pollution Prevention," *Pollution Prevention Review.* Summer 1993.

II.

ENVIRONMENTAL ACCOUNTING CASE STUDY: AMOCO YORKTOWN REFINERY

By Miriam Heller, David Shields, and Beth Beloff

1. Introduction

1.1 Amoco Oil Company

The Amoco Corporation is a worldwide integrated petroleum and chemical company. Amoco Oil Company is one of three major operating companies of the corporation. *(See Figure 11.)* In 1993, the Amoco Corporation earned $826 million through refining, marketing, and transportation on $10.8 billion in sales of refined products worldwide.[1] It is currently undergoing a major restructuring that will emphasize 17 newly formed business groups.

This case study centered on environmental costs at the Yorktown Refinery in Virginia. It did not consider the experience of Amoco Oil at other refineries, nor did it consider possible implications for the Amoco Production Company or the Amoco Chemical Company. Nonetheless, it is important to recognize that the consolidated financial entity is the Amoco Corporation.

At the end of 1993, Amoco Oil Company operated five refineries in the United States, with a total capacity of slightly less than 1 million barrels a day. In that year Amoco refineries averaged nearly 97 percent capacity utilization. Among U.S. refiners, Amoco ranked third in total volume, and markets about 6 percent of the refined products sold in the country.[2]

The petroleum industry in general, and the refining sector in particular, can anticipate significant changes over the next several

CASE HIGHLIGHTS: AMOCO YORKTOWN REFINERY

Amoco Oil Company's Yorktown Refinery, like the refining industry as a whole, faces significant environmental costs, both as a producer of petroleum products and as a source of pollution. This case study underscores the importance of identifying and tracking environmental costs to better understand how much is being spent and why.

Accounting for environmental costs in a highly integrated refinery is especially complex. Early on, the investigators explored the possibility of tracing environmental costs to process units. But it became clear that assigning costs at this level could lead to decisions with adverse economic and environmental consequences for both the refinery and the company because the effects of process-unit decisions are felt both upstream and downstream. For example, the decision to treat wastewater treatment sludge in a coker, while reducing off-site disposal costs, reduced yields of intermediate products and resulted in costly unanticipated shutdowns for cleaning and maintenance.

This study was valuable in revealing just how significant environmental costs are at Yorktown. The initial informal estimate of annual environmental costs was 3 percent of non-crude operating costs. After six months of study, they were found to be approximately 22 percent of non-crude operating costs. And even this understates the total, which would also include estimates of future environmental liabilities.

This study has also provided insights into where environmental costs arise. For example, maintenance costs are estimated to be over 15 percent of total environmental costs. This percentage is much higher than the cost of wastewater treatment, which had originally been considered one of the most significant environmental costs at the refinery. This case study also considered the relevance of environmental cost information in complex product mix decisions.

—*The editors*

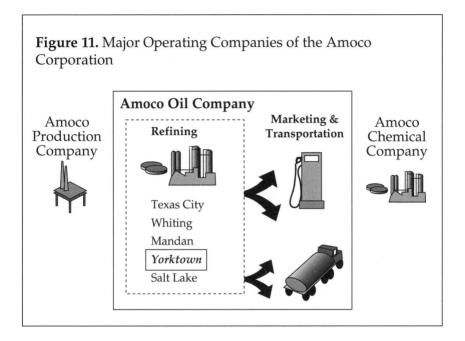

Figure 11. Major Operating Companies of the Amoco Corporation

years. There is a growing awareness of the importance of environmental performance to the overall economic performance of the industry.[3] In a letter to all employees, William D. Ford, President of Amoco Oil Company, wrote:

> [W]e are facing tremendous financial challenges caused by flat demand for our products, heavy capital requirements, and stringent and costly government regulation of our operations.... Some of you may think that—although the organization is changing now—demand will soon pick up, the regulatory environment will ease, costs will go down, and we'll be able to go back to business as usual. But I caution you not to think that way, because "business as usual" really is gone.[4]

1.2 The Yorktown Refinery

Despite its small size (53,000 barrels per day) relative to the facilities at Texas City (433,000 barrels) and Whiting (370,000 barrels), the Yorktown Refinery is considered a "complex" refinery.[5] It makes an especially rich subject for this case study because it was the setting for the unprecedented Amoco/Environmental Protection Agency (EPA) Pollution Prevention Project.[6] Conducted over two years at a cost of $2.3 million, this unique collaborative project quantified air emissions, water discharges, and other wastes generated at the facility. More important, it identified a range of options for preventing these releases, some of which appeared more cost-effective than those required by existing rules. The Amoco/EPA study not only created a wealth of information about environmental and economic aspects of refinery operations, it has also fueled interest in regulatory reform to encourage and reward the search for environmental improvements.

The Yorktown Refinery 1993 Strategic Plan recognizes the goal of improved performance through more cost-effective waste management and environmental compliance. For major environmental projects, the refinery seeks "to design, install, and commission facilities to meet regulatory requirements in a cost-effective manner."[7] They have instituted a waste minimization measure as part of the employee compensation program.

1.3 Case Study Focus

Petroleum refining is characterized by near-total integration among the many process units, which complicates the identification and attribution of environmental costs. Some portion of every barrel of crude may pass through each of the process units. Changes in one unit can affect others, both upstream and downstream. This high level of integration, combined with the distribution of decision-making authority, tends to reduce the relevance to decisions at the process level of even the best information on environmental costs and risks. So, efforts to reduce overall costs must cover the entire refining process, rather than just focusing on individual process units.

Integration this extreme posed obstacles to the early focus on specific products and processes. At the outset, the project team considered four potential perspectives on accounting for environmental costs. One alternative was to trace environmental costs to products; this was rejected because the inherent interdependence of refined products makes it impossible to isolate any single product. A second approach was to trace environmental costs to raw materials to determine whether they would change decisions about raw materials selection; this was rejected for this particular study because the selection and scheduling of the various crudes involves considerations across the Amoco Oil refineries.

The third alternative was to trace environmental costs to capital project decisions. Capital expenditures for environmental compliance have a considerable impact on refinery operations and costs. These represent only a part of total environmental costs, however. Furthermore, for large capital projects, attempts are usually made to identify significant costs associated with each alternative, regardless of whether they are labeled "environmental" or not. For these reasons, we chose not to focus on capital project evaluation or budgeting.

The fourth approach was to trace environmental costs to a specific unit or process within the refinery. The team chose to use a process focus to supplement other World Resources Institute case studies that center on products. After considering a number of processes, Amoco and the team selected the coker for closer investigation. The coker converts heavy petroleum residues into more valuable light products and coke, a low-grade solid fuel. In 1988, Amoco began injecting wastewater treatment sludge and other hazardous wastes into the coker, destroying the solid wastes and reducing the costs of off-site disposal. This allowed the company to close an on-site land farming operation. It also reduced the yield of valuable intermediate products, however, and resulted in higher maintenance requirements.

During the study, the team found little evidence that environmental cost information was relevant for decisions about the coker, which, like the on-site wastewater treatment plant, is a cost center and does not charge other process units.[8] Thus, better information on the environmental costs of coking would not have a clear impact on process-level decisions. Furthermore, an isolated focus on the coker ignored technical, environmental, and economic impacts upstream and downstream. So the focus was broadened from evaluating environmental costs at the process unit to approaching environmental cost accounting on a refinery-wide basis. Ironically, the findings indicate the value of linking environmental costs with products, raw materials, and capital decisions.

2. Petroleum Refining

2.1 Basics of the Refining Process
This overview shows the unique characteristics of petroleum refining, which can bear directly on environmental issues and accounting practices.

Petroleum refining uses a series of separation and reaction processes to transform crude oil and natural gas into a mix of gaseous, liquid, and solid petroleum products. At most refineries, crude oil arrives by pipeline, or sometimes by barge or ship, and it is stored in expansive tankage systems to await refining. Superimposed on these unit operations are process control systems to manipulate conditions (such as flow, temperature, and pressure) during start-up, operation, shutdown, and upsets, plus safety systems and pollution control systems (including scrubbers, flares, and wastewater treatment units) designed to assure environmental compliance.

The process of refining is based on the cracking of diverse hydrocarbon components into lighter liquids and gases, and separation of the fractions into more homogeneous mixtures. Separation typically occurs according to the boiling points of the components. The lightest fractions have lower boiling points and come off first. These fractions of light and heavy naphtha are eventually combined to produce gasoline. At higher temperatures, distillates such as jet fuels, kerosene, diesel fuels, and fuel oils separate out. Higher-value products can be recovered from the residuals, but only at additional cost. Petroleum coke, a solid hydrocarbon product, can be marketed as a low-value residual fuel. All the separation and cracking processes have large fuel and utility requirements.

Refined petroleum products, as a result of their heterogeneous compositions, are defined not by specific chemical composition but according to bulk characteristics, including octane rating, density, boiling range, volatility, and various discretionary specifications defined by distributors, consumers, and standards-setting organizations. They range from very light fuel gas, such as propane, through automotive and aviation gasolines, jet fuel, furnace oil, diesel fuel, and lubricants to heavy residual fuel oils, asphalt, and petroleum coke.[9]

2.2 Yorktown Refinery Processes

The Yorktown Refinery processes a variety of crude feedstocks, including high-sulfur Mayan crude from Mexico and low-sulfur crude from the North Sea. Crude oil arrives by ship or barge at the marine loading bay on the York River, where it is unloaded into tanks that can hold enough for roughly a week of operation. Yorktown's principal products are gasoline, heating oil, liquefied petroleum gas, and coke. The primary process units form a single train at the refinery. Crude petroleum oil enters the refining process at the combination unit. This consists of a crude desalting unit for removing entrained saltwater and dirt and a distillation unit for separating the crude into gasolines, distillates, and residual fuel oils.

Residual fuel oils and some heavy intermediates are routed to the coker for thermal cracking into higher valued, lighter products and petroleum coke. Although the purest grades of coke can be used in the manufacture of aluminum anodes, graphite, and carbides, the high-sulfur coke produced at Yorktown has a limited market. The heaviest liquid streams are recycled back to the coker. Heavy gas oils exiting the combination unit and the coker are returned to the fluid catalytic cracking unit (the "cat cracker"). Compared with thermal cracking, catalytic cracking yields higher octane gasoline but carries higher costs due to the disposal of spent catalysts.

The Yorktown Refinery also includes an Ultraformer unit for catalytically transforming naphthenes into aromatics that boost the octane rating of gasoline; an ethyl tertiary butyl ether (ETBE) unit for oxygenated gasoline production; a polymerization unit to increase the gasoline yield by combining some of the gaseous light hydrocarbons; alkylation units for combining lighter hydrocarbons into high-quality gasoline-blending compounds that boost octane; a distillate desulfurizer to remove potentially corrosive sulfur (which can interfere with catalysts, form hydrogen sulfide, and lower octane); a sulfur recovery unit; and a unit for treating fuel gas.

2.3 Product Slate Decisions

Market demand, product margins, transportation costs, refinery technology and vintage, and the price and availability of crude oil are some of the factors that affect decisions about what each refinery will produce. Large petroleum companies select a product slate taking into account corporate strategies across multiple refineries and their markets. As a vertically integrated firm, Amoco Corporation must weigh the impacts of refining decisions on both their upstream crude oil production company and their downstream chemical company.

Demand for refined product is seasonal, swinging between higher consumption of gasoline in the summer and of heating oil in the winter. Variations in feedstocks and products require that refineries be designed and operated with adequate flexibility. The refinery must also keep an eye on long-term trends in demand. The industry is highly competitive and offers individual companies little control over the market price of its products. Consequently, great emphasis is placed on driving down costs.

Crude oil prices and availability also enter into product decisions and affect refinery design and operations. During the past two decades the price of crude has swung from $3 per barrel to more than $30. Responding to the higher price of sweet crude and the increased demand for such lighter products as gasoline, diesel, and jet fuels, many refiners invested heavily to upgrade processing capacity in order to convert more lower cost, heavier, higher sulfur crudes into high-quality products.

Major changes in the composition of fuels, especially gasoline, during the past two decades have also had a great influence. Environmental regulations have a significant impact on the product slate. With the phaseout of lead in the 1980s, unit processes that produce octane-boosting aromatics such as benzene, toluene, and xylenes became more widespread. There has also been greater use of oxygenated fuels; blended with gasoline, oxygenates such as ETBE curb emissions of unburned hydrocarbons and carbon monoxide by promoting more complete combustion.

The refining industry bears the burden for changing fuels and related refinery redesign, estimated at $32 billion a year for reformulated gasoline, $3.3 billion for low-sulfur diesel fuels, and $670 million for oxygenated fuels.[10] The Yorktown Refinery is already equipped to produce ETBE. The refinery has also invested in technology for refining high-sulfur crudes and is prepared to meet additional regulatory requirements for low-sulfur diesel fuel.

As noted earlier, even relatively small petroleum refineries contain a tightly integrated series of process units with complex feedback loops. A particular product, such as premium unleaded gasoline, is a mixture of hydrocarbons from the crude unit, the cat cracker, the polymerization unit, and the ETBE unit. As a consequence, there is no single, well-defined product cost. Unlike a hypothetical widget manufacturer, decisions on the product slate cannot rest on the comparison of individual product margins. This can also complicate other decisions, such as whether to run more crude or purchase intermediates for further refining.

Despite all the complexities and uncertainties, refineries must choose a product mix. In practice, they take the prices of crude feedstocks and refined products as given and attempt to achieve a product slate that maximizes net earnings. Of course, this is subject to a host of constraints imposed by the available technology, by logistics (proximity of refineries to market and available transportation systems), and by the time required to make major process changes. At Yorktown, an important tool used to meet a given product slate is a linear programming model known as the Refinery Operating Plan (ROP).

To be practical, the ROP has a very simplified representation of the technical details of the refinery. It combines operational information from refineries (e.g., maintenance schedules, current operating capacities) with information on prices and characteristics of various crudes and the prices and demand for products from a planning group in the Chicago headquarters. In practice, the product slate is determined through an iterative process between these offices and refinery management.

The ROP in use at the Yorktown Refinery was developed in the early 1990s. Rather than attempting to capture all costs of production, it excludes costs that are expected to remain fixed with a changing product slate. Although Amoco believes that the choice of crude oil has a significant effect on environmental costs, this study raised the question of whether the cost structure imbedded in the ROP reflects the effect of product mix on environmental costs. (Although the project team did not review the detailed assumptions and structure of the ROP, Section 4 addresses the potential relevance of environmental cost information for the ROP.)

3. Environmental Issues

3.1 Yorktown Refinery Releases

Petroleum refining creates air emissions, water discharges, and solid wastes. One important set of pollution issues at refineries—notably sulfur, salts (brine), and metals—are the direct result of crude oil impurities separated in the refining process. Others, most notably volatile organic compound (VOC) emissions, represent a loss of potential product.

The most thorough inventory of releases derives from the Amoco/EPA Pollution Prevention Project, which involved an extensive and expensive multimedia sampling effort. Figure 12 presents the flow diagram for Yorktown with release sources. Recent emission updates indicate that the refinery generates 22,104 tons a year of polluting materials, releasing 9,980 tons to all environmental media.[11] These represent approximately 0.7 percent and 0.3 percent, respectively, of the total crude input, depending on crude composition and density. To put the emissions in perspective, Yorktown, the only petroleum refinery in Virginia, was not among the state's 10 highest emitters of toxic chemicals.

3.2 Air Emissions and Control

The vast majority of releases at Yorktown are to the atmosphere, with two-thirds (by weight) exiting stacks, flares, and other point sources and about a quarter of the total released as fugitive emissions. The Amoco/EPA study focused on refinery air emissions, in part as a result of new air pollution regulations that are drastically affecting refinery operations. The Clean Air Act Amendments of 1990 constitute the most far-reaching legislation ever to affect the refining industry. Implementing regulations will have an impact on the industry, both as a stationary source and as a producer of a regulated product. They will affect the distribution system, since product quality standards depend on regional ambient air quality, as well as demand for gasoline. Refineries will face stricter requirements on VOCs, air toxics, and fugitive emissions. In addition, permitting requirements and enforcement procedures are likely to change in ways that are difficult to predict.

Figure 12. Yorktown Refinery Flow Diagram with Release Sources [Amoco/U.S. EPA, 1992]

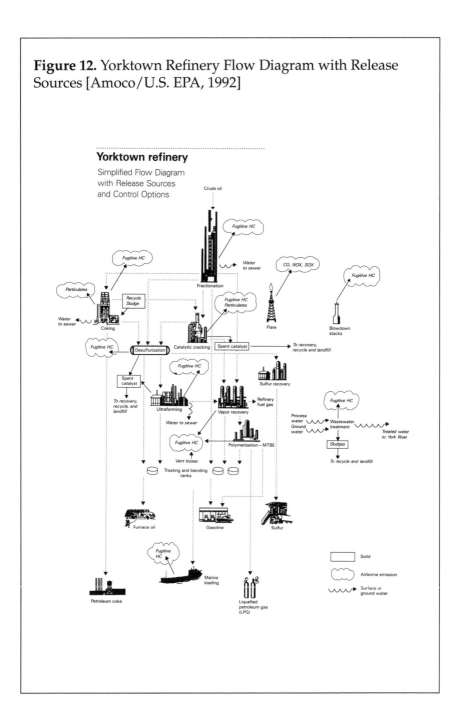

3.3 Water Treatment and Discharge

At the Yorktown Refinery, liquid wastes from process areas are collected in the sewer system for treatment. The collection system merges after exiting the process areas and before entering the wastewater treatment plant, a facility shared by all process units. The wastewater treatment facility does not track contributions by individual units. Consequently, process units are not charged for water usage. This reflects common practice in the industry and is an outgrowth of the historical structure of process units as cost centers that send wastes downstream to end-of-pipe treatment and control facilities.[12]

Pending reauthorization of the Clean Water Act will present additional compliance issues for the petroleum industry. Stricter management of storm water, groundwater, and process wastewater could be required. The Great Lakes Initiative, which is geared toward zero toxic discharges, represents another development with relevance for water pollution and control. There is concern that if this becomes a model for the nation, even coastal facilities like the Yorktown Refinery could face much more stringent requirements.

3.4 Solid Waste Generation and Management

Solid wastes at the refinery range from spent catalyst to construction waste. By volume, hazardous sludges from the corrugated plate interceptor (CPI) separator and nonhazardous biological sludges from the wastewater treatment facility are the greatest contributors. Both of these are good examples of cross-media transfers. As the refinery moves toward higher effluent water quality, the end result is an increase in these solid wastes.

Information on solid and hazardous waste management forms the basis of the environmental component of Amoco's gain-sharing program, which provides a financial incentive to employees to reduce wastes. At Yorktown, this information is entered into an internal Waste Tracking Report system annually. Another Amoco system, the Environmental Reporting and Information Network, records waste according to on-site versus off-site management and provides cost estimates for managing the waste, including handling and transport. The system also provides specific data on waste disposed or incinerated off-site. It relies on a waste manifest program. Off-site waste management information can be obtained by the manifest system mandated under the Resource Conservation and Recovery Act (RCRA). On-site land disposal makes use of an internal manifest system. Internal costs are assigned to shipments going to landfill, such as sandblast grit, catalyst, refractory, and insulation. The wastes reported here are also included in the gain-sharing program.

In addition to the waste disposal options just discussed, hazardous CPI separator sludge, biological sludge from the wastewater treatment plant, some tank bottoms, monoethanolamine (MEA) reclaimer sludge from the gas treater, oil waste from cleaning and spills, liquid waste, and sludge from cleaning sewers are all sent to the coker for thermal treatment. The waste originating at the CPI separator is a listed hazardous waste. Biological sludge from the wastewater treatment plant is not considered hazardous. It would become so, however, if it is mixed with the CPI separator sludge prior to coking.

There are obvious, if not totally quantifiable, savings associated with avoiding land disposal and possible future liability. But there are also costs associated with coker injection. Coking wastes as performed at the Yorktown Refinery decreases the quality of the intermediate products (coker output). This is because the waste-coking process diverts drum capacity, decreases the efficiency of the coker since the watery sludges have higher heat requirements, results in increased coke production, and thereby shortens the time before coke drums are switched. The diminished quality of the coker output streams may also affect downstream processes such as the cat cracker. At the time of the study, the coker could not handle all the CPI separator sludge and biosludge. A process modification was under way to improve the efficiency of coking waste and free up additional capacity.

4. Accounting for Environmental Costs

4.1 Environmental Accounting and Organizational Issues
In a 1993 study, the National Petroleum Council estimated the costs of environmental regulation for refineries, both as stationary

sources and petroleum products producers, at \$152 billion be-
tween 1991–2010.[13] Some of these costs, especially those associated with reformulated and oxygenated fuels, may eventually be
passed on to consumers. Refiners unable to make the required
capital expenditures may be forced to shut down. The magnitude
of these estimates points to the importance of identifying and
tracking environmental costs. This will allow management to
adapt existing operating methods and procedures to meet required levels of compliance, as well as to improve operating efficiency. In addition, better accounting of costs can improve environmental management by providing better information for
routine and nonroutine decisions.

Amoco's internal efforts at environmental accounting at the
Yorktown Refinery demonstrate the feasibility of modifying existing
information systems to enhance current methods of tracking environmental costs. Changing the current accounting system to better
capture environmental costs will not in itself guarantee environmental cost control, however. Successful environmental management
will hinge on establishing a framework that directly links business
goals and environmental strategies to operational implementation
and that aids both cost management and decision-making.

The Strategy-Implementation Cycle in Figure 13 is offered as a
framework for viewing the organizational processes that must be
refined and integrated. This illustrates the interaction between
three sets of activities.

The strategy formulation function takes place at the upper levels of corporate management. It consists of taking stock of the current conditions facing the company (legal, economic, and regulatory), and the creation or modification of an operating plan to
maximize performance, given these conditions. The strategy formulation phase has been well-documented, and most companies
perform this function well.[14] The resulting strategy is translated
into corporate goals and objectives, and then into sub-unit goals
and objectives. These relate not only to profitability and line of business issues, but also to measurable responses to external challenges,
such as increasingly stringent environmental regulations. The sub-
unit goals and objectives are then reflected in the budget process.
Without funding, major operating objectives cannot be met.

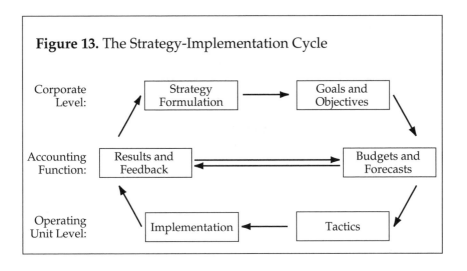

Figure 13. The Strategy-Implementation Cycle

Dropping down from the budget to the operating unit level, tactics refer to specific sets of activities that will be performed in order to meet the organizational goals and objectives. Although tactics will, to some degree, be developed at the corporate level, the portfolio of activities must be developed at the sub-unit level, where there is the most direct knowledge of infrastructure and staffing. The implementation step follows the tactics step, in that the activities selected are put into place, and non-financial monitoring of performance begins. At this stage, activities are modified through trial and error, in order to improve the effectiveness and efficiency of the process.

The implementation and tactics steps form an iterative process of planning and carrying out the activities that will operate the sub-unit in a manner consistent with stated organizational goals and objectives. But these are by necessity conflicting and impossible to satisfy totally. For example, firms have short-term profitability and longer-term growth goals that are usually quite ambitious, as well as environmental goals, community citizenship goals, and worker partnership goals. Yet there is an inherent conflict between maximizing short-run profit and making the investment in training, infrastructure, and customer markets that might result in long-run profitability. Another example is the inherent conflict between worker partnership goals and reducing costs through downsizing.

Finally, the results and feedback step consists of accounting and operational measurements of actual outcomes and comparison with anticipated levels of performance. The feedback linkage is strongest with the budget, in that deviations between actual and expected outcomes are first evaluated by operating personnel. A secondary feedback, primarily through measures of profitability, links results to the corporate functions of formulating strategy and setting organizational goals and objectives.

Although most companies perform each of the steps in the Strategy-Implementation Cycle quite well, the challenge is to integrate them all. Perhaps the most difficult linkage is between corporate goals and objectives and the plant-level tactics and implementation cycle. This gap is explained by differences in focus and in task. In terms of focus, corporate managers tend to have a relatively long time horizon, and are concerned with integrating the efforts of multiple operating levels in multiple locations. Plant-level personnel are more concerned with maintaining short-run profitability and with meeting short-run goals set at the corporate level.

In addition, the integration of the implementation step with results and feedback has historically been difficult. This is one reason for the recent popularity of Activity-Based Costing (ABC), in which cost allocations are driven from cost-generating activities in the company. Traditional cost accounting aggregates costs by cost type, and then allocates them across cost centers. This often results in inaccurate cost allocations, and provides management with relatively unreliable cost figures with which to make decisions.

Integration of these steps might be achieved by explicitly developing a portfolio of activities that are designed to satisfy the goals and objectives determined at the corporate level. These activities would form a basis for Activity-Based Costing and Activity-Based Management. Implementing ABC has many advantages for environmental cost accounting. First, it is easier for management to think about what environmental costs really are since costs are identified with the activities that actually cause them. Second, ABC provides a dollar quantification of activities, which can be used to assess the cost-benefit trade-off of portfolios of activities, and facilitates complete linkages within the Strategy-Implementation Cycle.

Yet the estimates of environmental costs presented in Section 4.3 do not emanate from a portfolio of environmental activities explicitly tied to organizational goals and objectives. Rather, they have been identified from the "results" section of the Strategy-Implementation Cycle. Although this is typical for cost aggregation by the financial function, it risks omitting the costs associated with some important activities. For example, if there are no cost pools associated with "community relations-environmental" or "lobbying-environmental," these items may be accidentally omitted from the environmental cost system. The problem would be remedied by continuing the analysis as follows:

1. Determine the current activities at the Yorktown Refinery that are intended to satisfy environmental goals and objectives. These activities need not be strictly environmental ones; those that are partially environmental should be flagged as such.

2. Determine appropriate cost drivers (measures of the cost-generating activity) for each activity or portfolio of activities.

3. Tie the current costs of these activities to them, to establish approximate current costs per unit of activity. These costs should be rolled up to determine total current environmental costs. In addition, the extent to which these costs are truly variable should be determined.

4. Conduct a review of each portfolio of activities; if there is no organizational goal or objective corresponding to a portfolio of activities, management must determine whether those activities should continue. Similarly, review each organizational goal and objective to determine if there is a portfolio of activities in place to implement it.

5. Institute an environmental cost report, in which the incremental (variable) and committed (fixed) current amounts are shown, and total environmental costs are reported. This report should include an identification of the portfolio of activities being performed, and the organizational goals and objectives being served. It should be circulated throughout the organization, and form a significant part of the annual review process.

4.2 Existing Accounting Information and Environmental Costs

The Yorktown Refinery does not have a dedicated environmental accounting system. Cost information was obtained from a number of distinct sources, including the General Financial System (GFS), which maintains the general ledger balances; the capital asset ledger; the Maintenance Management System (MMS); the 1993 budget; estimates from Economic and Scheduling; hydrocarbon loss information; and management's estimates from various refinery and general office staff department sources.

There is a clear interest at the corporate and refinery levels in having access to information on environmental costs. A number of other projects under way at Amoco address various aspects of environmental costs and management. At Yorktown, several managers expressed the view that the costs of environmental compliance are already high and growing. Some indicated that capital improvements for environmental compliance were driving out other opportunities for capital investment. The Amoco/EPA Project concluded that the current regulatory process tends to force Amoco and other companies to make environmental changes in unrealistically short periods of time, and with insufficient flexibility to find cost-effective solutions. Mandated technologies and short time frames can increase the costs of compliance substantially.

The investigation of environmental costs raises a number of practical questions:

- Which of the currently captured costs are identified as environmental?
- Are there important environmental costs that are not being captured at all?
- Is identifying environmental costs useful in project development, decision-making, and other managerial activities?
- To what extent are these environmental costs controllable?
- To what extent would assigning environmental costs to processes and products improve operating decisions?

Without relevance to decision-making, environmental accounting information may not be worth the cost required to gather and evaluate it. Refinery management is motivated by achieving satisfactory profits and cash flow. To the extent that capturing environmental costs and benefits may significantly improve operating decisions, such information is useful. But if the information is not an important input into any management decision, or if it does not provide operational feedback that in some way influences employee behavior, it is probably not worth gathering.

An exception to this might be made for information that would help management participate in regulatory development. By gaining experience with environmental cost information now, companies will be better prepared to respond to new guidelines arising from industry associations, the accounting profession, or regulatory agencies. EPA and some state regulatory agencies have already indicated that accounting for environmental costs is an important element of waste minimization programs.

Determining which costs are environmental is not trivial. One commonly used method was presented in the EPA Pollution Prevention Benefits Manual.[15] This specifies four tiers of costs for use in evaluating pollution prevention alternatives:

Hierarchy of Environmental Costs

Tier 0: Direct costs associated with capital expenditures, raw materials, other operating and maintenance costs, etc.

Tier 1: Hidden regulatory costs from activities such as monitoring and reporting, etc.

Tier 2: Contingent liabilities arising from remediation of contaminated sites, fines and penalties for noncompliance, etc.

Tier 3: Less tangible costs and benefits from consumer perceptions, employee and community relations, etc.

This classification is useful in approaching environmental costs for two reasons. First, it is appealing to categorize environmental costs in terms of the activity that creates them. Second, the categorization has gained a degree of acceptance in a field where definitions have yet to be standardized. The EPA Manual recommends that technologies or investment decisions are first evaluated on the basis of Tier 0. Subsequent tiers are evaluated only so long as pollution-prevention alternatives continue to appear not to be cost-effective. If an investment option fails after including Tier 3 costs, it is viewed as not cost-effective.

4.3 Examination of Environmental Costs

The initial approach to environmental cost accounting entailed analyzing accounts contained in the GFS system and determining whether the costs were environmental. This information was supplemented by other sources such as the MMS. The costs were then added to a tally. This section builds on those efforts to assemble for the first time the costs associated with a wide range of environmental issues facing Amoco's Yorktown Refinery.

At most petroleum refineries, operating costs are dominated by crude oil. Since even small fluctuations in the price of crude can overshadow the operating costs of refining, it is customary to track costs at the refinery level exclusive of the costs of feedstock. In this report, all "non-crude operating costs" refers to the refinery operating costs less the cost of crude oil and other petroleum feedstocks.

The estimate of aggregate environmental costs is illuminating in its own right. Total environmentally related costs at the Yorktown Refinery were estimated to be 21.9 percent of total non-crude operating costs in 1993. And the tally of environmental costs is not yet complete.

The results also provide interesting, and somewhat unexpected, insights into where these costs arise. Although the primary approach taken in identifying the environmental costs was account analysis, the results also reflect a number of identifiable environmental activities and their costs. Simply knowing the total expenditures for environmental issues does not necessarily lead to a decision on how to manage or reduce them, however. This question of the use of environmental cost information at the Yorktown Refinery is considered in more detail in Section 4.4. The remainder of this section is devoted to more specific findings from Amoco's efforts to account for environmental costs at that refinery.

The accounting system may not adequately capture the true nature of environmental costs. In the refinery, some costs, such as those directly related to a wastewater treatment plant, could be categorized as environmental. Others are commingled in cost pools with non-environmental items. For example, only a portion of maintenance costs are environmental. To the extent that there is no breakdown in a given cost pool, the amounts associated with environmental items are difficult to determine. This complicates the accurate allocation of environmental cost to products.

Even if environmental costs can be separated, it is still difficult to trace them accurately to product or process. Indirect costs are routinely allocated by convenient measures of resource consumption, such as labor hours, machine hours, or production units. To the extent that different products incur different environmental costs, these methods distort estimates of product and process costs. In fact, defining product cost is difficult in petroleum refining regardless of the environmental share.

As discussed in Section 4.1, an Activity-Based Costing approach, in which environmental activities are identified and tied to costs, can help overcome allocation problems, and may facilitate better definition of cost pools and appropriate drivers. In addition, by identifying the activities that incur costs, management has an important tool for cost management.

Although cost estimates were derived from an account analysis approach, the project has benefited from ABC concepts. This work has already resulted in better identification of actual environmental outlays and supplemented the data available in existing cost systems. Of total recurring costs deemed "environmental," approximately 40 percent are already charged to the responsible process. The remainder are divided evenly between charges to overhead cost centers and charges to on-site waste treatment cost centers.

In generating these estimates, refinery activities that incur environmental costs were identified. Then costs found in the accounting system were extracted using either elements of expense or charge codes. In some cases, a single element of expense related to environmental expenses only (e.g., those associated with the wastewater treatment plant). For costs that were pooled within an expense element, other methods of estimating the costs were required. Some such costs could be extracted using other information systems. For example, the automated MMS tracks work orders. By flagging individual work orders as environmental or both environment and safety, maintenance costs associated with environmental activities could be assessed. Where no other documented source of information existed, refinery management and staff estimated the portion of pooled costs that were driven by environmental concerns.

The costs estimated during this project can be viewed within the hierarchy of costs given earlier. The current estimates focus primarily on Tier 0—capital, operating and maintenance costs. Some estimates of Tier 1 costs are also included. Some of the 21.9 percent of non-crude operating costs match conventional notions of environmental costs. For example, the costs of pollution control are primarily in Tier 0. The wastewater treatment plant incurred total expenses of 1.4 percent of non-crude operating costs, or only about 6 percent of total environmental costs.

These most obvious environmental costs likely formed the basis for an earlier, informal estimate of 3 percent of non-crude operating costs provided by the Environmental Health and Safety staff during the site visit. This is an indication of how difficult it is, even for knowledgeable "insiders," to identify environmental costs within a complex industrial operation such as a petroleum refinery. The contrast between this figure and the magnitude of the figures in Table 4 indicates the value to both Yorktown Refinery and

Table 4. Summary of Environmental Costs at the Yorktown Refinery, 1993 Expressed as a Percentage of Non-crude Operating Costs

Waste Treatment	4.9 percent
Maintenance	3.3 percent
Product Requirements	2.7 percent
Depreciation	2.5 percent
Administration, Compliance	2.4 percent
Sulfur Recovery	1.1 percent
Waste Disposal	0.7 percent
Fees, Fines, Penalties	0.2 percent
Total Recurring Costs	17.9 percent
Total Non-Recurring Costs	4.0 percent
Total Costs	21.9 percent

Amoco Oil Company management of deriving better estimates of environmental costs.

Some environmental costs are not explicitly defined in the accounting system but are aggregated in cost pools. For example, maintenance costs were estimated to be 3.3 percent of non-crude operating costs, or more than 15 percent of total environmental costs. This was dramatically higher than the cost of waste disposal and of fees, fines, and penalties combined. So neither the amount nor the identity of Tier 0 costs is necessarily obvious.

One difficulty in breaking down cost pools is the distinction between environmental and closely related costs. Sometimes it is not possible to separate these. For instance, as part of the environmental cost assessment, Amoco flagged some costs in the MMS as "environmental" and others as "environmental/safety." Also, since these labels are not systematically employed, the actual costs of environmentally related maintenance may be understated.

The value of product loss was estimated to be 0.8 percent of non-crude operating costs. This, however, was not considered an environmental cost by Amoco. It is common practice for refiners to track overall loss of material in terms of quantity, since it translates into unconverted hydrocarbon and lost revenue. Product loss generally represents a low percentage of the total crude input, less than 0.3 percent at the Yorktown Refinery. However, due to the large throughputs of even small refineries, the benefits of hydrocarbon recovery can be significant.

A set of non-obvious Tier 0 costs relates to using the Yorktown coker for treatment of biosludge. The coker converts hazardous CPI separator sludge and non-hazardous biosludge to non-hazardous hydrocarbons, primarily petroleum coke. Coking the sludges offers clear savings, mostly in the form of reduced cost and future liability for off-site management. But it has both direct and indirect costs. Environmental cost accounting clarifies them, shedding new light on pollution-prevention decisions. This process penalty, the operation of the sludge facility, and the one-time shutdown amounted to more than $2 million. By 1994, this cost had been significantly reduced.

Some of the hidden costs of regulatory compliance, indicated in Tier 1, are included in the current environmental cost estimates. For example, staff dedicated to ensuring compliance, monitoring, inspections, and lab services fall into this category. Other Tier 1 costs are industry-specific. Notably, 2.7 percent of non-crude operating costs, or about 12 percent of the total environmental costs, is attributed to compliance with environmental regulations on product specifications (e.g., oxygenated gasoline and volatility). This includes only costs that do not add product value. Although the cost hierarchy provides for these costs, they are obviously industry-specific and will require greater analysis to define. They are potentially important since they provide partial evidence of the unequal regulatory burden imposed by regulations. In addition, industry-specific operating methods and issues point to the need for industry-specific treatment of environmental cost accounting methods and practices.

Some costs that are currently insignificant could grow large with changes in management strategies and regulations. For example, the costs of environmental auditing and training may increase substantially. Tracking such costs systematically serves the important purpose of directing attention to trends and helps managers anticipate and respond to such changes. Otherwise, management may attempt to optimize environmental activity with an incomplete understanding of the costs. More thorough auditing may uncover ways to reduce defined environmental costs; anticipated savings would be overestimated if the environmental cost savings did not identify the cost of the incremental environmental auditing.

Tier 2 costs, such as fines, penalties, future remediation costs, property damage, and the cost of eventual liability, are challenging to assess. The estimates here do not include such costs with the exception of fines and penalties. Estimating them is inherently uncertain due to future regulatory changes and many other factors. In the current estimate of environmental costs at Yorktown, remediation expenses appear under "non-recurring costs." However, the costs of future liabilities are not included. Amoco is currently reviewing methods for estimating this. In view of the potential costs involved, the Yorktown Refinery has reduced off-site treatment and disposal significantly in recent years.

At this stage, significant Tier 3 costs, the less tangible future costs and benefits, have not been incorporated. These are extremely difficult to estimate in terms of how large they will be, in what units they will be measured, and at what time in the future they will be incurred. They are real costs, nonetheless, that may significantly influence decision-making when they are recognized. Examples include community and employee relations.

As environmental costs are identified, it is important to understand the behavior of the costs as volume or activity levels change. Regardless of whether the existing accounting system currently classifies them as fixed or variable, particular attention should be paid to accurately characterizing the true behavior of these costs. Incorrect classification can lead to incorrect cost projections, which in turn can affect capital project and other decisions.

Amoco's accounting of environmental costs at Yorktown distinguished between fixed, variable, and programmed costs. Programmed costs are those that vary, but not directly with production. For the environmental cost assessment, Amoco opted to distinguish between regular on-going expenses and nonrecurring expenses, such as coker shutdown due to sludge injection. This breakdown will allow analysis of which costs vary proportionally with effluent and emissions and can therefore be expected to decline with waste reduction, and which ones may not always be anticipated or controllable. Amoco observed, nonetheless, that many of the recurring costs vary more directly with regulatory requirements than with waste generation. Additional regulations can add layers of company-wide reporting requirements, as well as significant investments in additional technology. Such requirements result in additional fixed costs, which can dominate the variable cost component associated with waste generation. Thus, the ability to anticipate or influence new regulations may determine the degree to which costs can be controlled.

4.4 Uses of Environmental Cost Information

Amoco has made significant progress in identifying and understanding environmental costs at the Yorktown Refinery. In part, this reflects the company's commitment to meet the challenges of environmental compliance creatively without abandoning business objectives. The success of this effort also reflects on the importance of personnel who can integrate financial, managerial, legal, and technical issues to arrive at the best solution.

Decision Support

Because of the highly interdependent nature of the various units in petroleum refining, it is impossible to anticipate fully the cost implications of process changes. For instance, the coking of biosludges and hazardous wastes resulted in a series of unexpected costs. Excess water and lower heat content from the coking operation reduced the value of the intermediate product mix, "penalizing" the process. In addition, the process resulted in an unanticipated buildup of solids in the equipment. As a result, shutdowns (or outages) were necessary to clean and maintain the coker. Table 5 illustrates how Amoco's understanding of these and other potential costs expanded in several key decisions over several years.

Although even the best accounting information could not have foreseen all these costs, recognizing how the coking of wastes contributes to various costs is necessary to understanding—and man-

Table 5. Evolution of Cost Considerations in the Coking of Waste at Yorktown

Costs	1987 Decision to Coke Waste	1991 Coker Upgrade	1993 Coker Upgrade
Capital	$	$	$
Operating	$	$	$
Coker Outages	–	$	$
Maintenance	✓	✓	$
Process Penalty	✓	✓	$
Permitting	✓	✓	✓
Product Certification	✓	✓	✓
Compliance, Record-keeping	–	✓	✓
Public, Govt. Relations	–	–	–
Fines, Penalties	–	–	–
Future Liability	–	–	–

Key: $ costs considered and quantified
✓ costs considered but not quantified
– costs judged insignificant or not recognized

aging—these costs. Still, many complex and even site-specific factors make it difficult to anticipate the magnitude of environmental costs. For example, the shutdown of the coker was accommodated quickly so that only a few days of coker throughput were lost. Had a longer shutdown been required, tankage capacity would have been exceeded and refinery production affected—with much larger cost impacts. In this case, the more detailed appreciation of costs supports the original decision to coke wastes on site.

The Refinery Operating Plan, as discussed in Section 2.3, offers another example of how environmental cost information can feed into management decision-making. The ROP reportedly treats all environmental costs as fixed costs. However, it is clear from Amoco's internal identification of environmental costs that at least some of these are variable. Thus, actual cost levels may be changing as product slate, feedstock, or output levels vary, but this change is not reflected in the ROP. This may result in decisions that are not optimal. A second reason the ROP may fall short is that current refining models do not accurately account for the costs of waste production.

The use of environmental costs in capital budgeting decisions can improve decision-making. For example, the Amoco/EPA Project examined various possibilities for controlling VOC emissions from the coker blowdown pond. The project had identified the pond as a significant source of benzene release. Amoco planned to enclose it at a cost of $2 million. On closer inspection, refinery staff determined that they could eliminate the blowdown pond altogether for just $50,000. This is an example of how the economics of pollution prevention can change dramatically with different "technology." And how, given output targets, accounting information, and adequate time, industry can reach better solutions at lower cost than might be realized through mandated process regulation.

This experience also shows how investment in research and development can be guided by environmental cost accounting. New pollution prevention technology (or technology with pollution prevention as a side benefit) will be more likely to be implemented if environmental costs are recognized. Design practices will be more likely to incorporate low-emissions options given this information. Investments in monitoring and waste-handling systems will become more prudent after taking into account the full costs of the alternatives. In addition, siting decisions for production and storage facilities will improve if the financial implications of alternative locations are taken into account.

A more accurate picture of environmental costs will obviously provide a better estimate of how those costs change in line with new government regulations. By tracking these costs more accurately, the precision of future environmental cost forecasts can be improved along with the estimates of the impacts of regulations. This may facilitate a more proactive outlook by companies such as Amoco, as they face ever more stringent regulations.

Monitoring and Directing Attention

Knowledge of the environmental costs at the Yorktown Refinery is useful as an attention-directing device, both at the refinery and the corporate level. Managers are better able to grasp and identify the importance of tangible, quantified information than of intangible, qualitative estimates. The absolute magnitude and source of environmental costs can highlight the significance of environmental management issues. As noted, this investigation found that total environmental costs at the Yorktown Refinery were 21.9 percent of non-crude operating costs in 1993. This is only a small fraction of the price per gallon of refined product. However, it is well over three times the estimated 1993 earnings for that refinery.

Another potential attention-directing use of environmental cost arises in the case of post-investment assessment. Companies frequently implement capital-intensive projects or make changes in process technology without tracking the subsequent performance of the project or investment. A post-investment assessment measures the effectiveness of decision-making and business processes after the fact. This feedback is essential for continuous improvement, which could be measured against an internal as well as an external yardstick. Integrating environmental costs into this sort of decision framework could provide the foundation for analyzing internal decision-making performance. It would provide a baseline against which a corporation could measure its decision-making and business process effectiveness relative to its competitors, and could be extended to incorporate the effects of current or proposed legislation and regulation.

Motivation and Managerial Control

Environmental costs can positively affect managers' motivation and behavior by adjusting the reward system to take environmental issues into account at an appropriate level. For example, Amoco currently maintains a Variable Incentive Plan, which is a gain-sharing plan that incorporates waste minimization as an integral part of an overall employee performance rating. The program provides Amoco employees with cash payout opportunities based on a number of performance measures addressing issues such as safety, waste generation, refinery yield, product quality, energy usage, and product recovery.

The gain-sharing system encourages and rewards the identification of pollution prevention alternatives. At Yorktown, waste management constitutes 50 percent of the gain-sharing variable. This targets many on-site, off-site, and recycled wastes on a tonnage basis. These wastes are primarily from spent catalysts and spills. Remediation associated with historical pollution activities is excluded to avoid penalizing the current work force for past practices. The waste generation metric also exempts concrete wastes that are landfilled on-site, wastes from emptying and cleaning out of bulk storage tanks, and waste injected into the coker. Clearly, this last feature has the effect of encouraging the coking of sludges over off-site management.

The Yorktown Refinery does have a number of waste-reduction success stories, some of which demonstrate the usefulness of tying costs to activities in order to manage costs. High tank-turnaround costs led individuals to take the initiative that resulted in modification of the sandblast grit procedure. The newer procedure resulted in a reduction of waste from 100 tons to 10. Once Amoco noticed that MEA reclaimer sludge had a significantly negative impact on the cost of coking, they discovered that the MEA was being changed out long before it was necessary.[16]

There are limitations to the usefulness of allocating costs (including environmental costs) to individual processes within the refinery, however. As this case study revealed, it is unwise to allocate costs to the coker level because few decisions can be made there without affecting upstream and downstream processes. If the coker operation is optimized through the use of allocated costs, this may be less than optimal for the refinery as a whole because the resulting costs will be assigned to upstream and downstream processes. If these costs exceed the savings generated through coker optimization, the refinery as a whole will not have benefited. In general, an operating decision should be made at a level where all measurable effects of the decision are experienced. At Yorktown, this means that coker operating decisions (beyond housekeeping decisions) should be made at the refinery level.

It is also worth considering whether it is appropriate to "ignore" some costs because they are externally imposed (and, hence, out of the refinery's control). For example, the environmental costs associated with producing low-sulfur diesel fuels were not included in the tally of environmental costs. This is because Amoco opted to charge the incremental cost (which was approximately offset by the higher price at the pump for low-sulfur diesel) to Amoco Oil Marketing. Thus Amoco Oil Marketing's profit is unaffected by product mix. The marketing group has a similar arrangement for the costs of producing oxygenated gasolines. Since the marketing group provides input to the product slate, they have some degree of control over product mix and, hence, its profitability. However, the refinery should be held accountable for costs of production, whether externally imposed or not.

5. Summary and Recommendations

Amoco Oil Company's Yorktown Refinery, like the refining industry as a whole, faces significant environmental costs which are likely to grow with increasingly strict regulations. This case study underscores the importance of identifying and tracking environmental costs in order to better understand how much is being spent and why. This in turn will facilitate better management of environmental costs and help ensure that maximum environmental benefit is obtained at minimum cost.

An overarching issue concerns the relationship between corporate goals and objectives at the highest level of the Amoco Oil Company and their implementation at the refinery. Amoco Corporation is responsible for formulating strategy and for determining the organizational goals and objectives to be pursued by the entire company. These are then translated into operating objectives for the various sub-units.

One set of goals and objectives relates to environmental performance at the refineries, where they are redefined into the tactics and implementation steps necessary to fulfill the environmental objectives of the corporation. At Amoco, these goals and objectives are clearly communicated to the refineries, and the refineries are expected to implement activities for fulfilling them.

Although environmental, health, and safety goals are a top priority throughout the Amoco Oil Company, the cost of achieving them is not well known. As a result, environmental performance cannot be evaluated on equal terms with competing goals, some of which are more readily measured by the financial accounting system. By estimating current contributors to environmental costs and clearly identifying the objectives for which they are incurred, environmental performance can be tracked and evaluated in the same way as other business activities. While it is not necessary to build this into the managerial accounting system, an environmental cost system would make use of this information. In addition, such a system provides an important linkage between corporate goals and objectives and their implementation at the refinery level.

This case study also demonstrates that accounting for environmental costs in a refinery is not simple. The inherent complexity and integration of petroleum refining has important implications for the application of environmental accounting. For example, early on the case study explored the possibility of tracing environmental costs to process units. In a focus on activities with environmental significance at a single unit, it became clear that assigning environmental costs at this level could lead to decisions with adverse economic and environmental consequences for both the refinery and the company. This is because the effects of process unit decisions are felt both upstream and downstream. For example, the decision to treat wastewater treatment sludge in a coker, while reducing off-site disposal costs, resulted in costly unanticipated shutdowns for cleaning and maintenance.

In this particular case, the decision was still considered by Amoco to be the best solution, despite these additional costs. But this may not always be the case. For example, management noted that if the crude oil storage units are assigned the cost of disposing the solids that settle out in the tanks, this would provide an incentive to run mixers to keep these impurities in suspension. This would result in the waste being passed on to other parts of the refinery, where the costs of handling it could be much higher. This illustrates the importance of ensuring that the goals of local managers remain aligned with those of the whole organization once the allocation rules have been changed. This may necessitate a re-evaluation of performance-evaluation schemes, to prevent a situation where locally optimal decisions are encouraged at the expense of overall refinery operations.

In addition to the question of where environmental costs are allocated, there are important questions concerning the nature of these costs and their drivers. By definition, fixed costs are not susceptible to change over the short run. Therefore, decisions that seek to avoid allocated fixed costs will not result in overall cost avoidance for the company. However, this case study demonstrates that a number of important environmental costs are not fixed, suggesting the potential for cost reduction. While the classification of costs as fixed, variable, or programmed is useful for short-term decisions (e.g., operating and maintenance activities), it could discourage aggressive process or product redesign options. Fixed costs change in the long run, and programmed costs change at the discretion of management. In the long run, all costs are variable.

In view of the difficulties and complexities of accounting for environmental costs in a refinery, it is unlikely that a single accounting "system" could be devised that would be universally applicable throughout the refining industry. Each refinery will have different requirements depending on such factors as the company's environmental goals, the nature of existing information systems, and how the information is to be used.

The approach used in this study demonstrates the feasibility of using an existing information system to account for environmental costs. Although the primary source of information was derived from the General Financial System, other internal information sources such as Amoco's capital asset ledger and maintenance management system proved helpful in identifying and quantifying environmental costs.

Despite existing uncertainties and problems of definition, this study has been valuable in revealing just how significant environmental costs are at the Yorktown refinery. The initial, informal estimate of environmental costs was 3 percent of non-crude operating costs. After six months of study, environmental costs were found to be approximately 22 percent of non-crude operating costs. And even this understates the total costs, in that it does not include estimates of unknown future environmental liabilities—for example, from waste disposal. The magnitude of environmental costs at the Yorktown refinery is sufficient justification in itself for Amoco to continue to identify and track environmental costs. Amoco should also take advantage of its on-going efforts to identify and quantify future environmental liabilities, and incorporate these estimates into existing financial systems.

This study has also provided insights into where environmental costs arise. For example, maintenance costs are estimated to be over 15 percent of total environmental costs. This is much higher than the cost of wastewater treatment, which had originally been considered one of the most significant environmental costs at the refinery. Both the nature and magnitude of these environmental costs justify greater management attention to current cost levels, and to methods to reduce them. This may extend to process re-design or to adjustment of production decisions. Environmental accounting can also draw attention to everyday operations that are considered peripheral to refinery operations but that may have critical impacts on future environmental costs.

The relevance of environmental cost information on product mix decisions was considered in this case study. These decisions are made above the refinery level, based on factors such as customer demand and profit margins. Once the product mix has been selected, the Refinery Operating Plan translates this into detailed operating parameters for the various units. However, it is not clear whether environmental costs are considered in this process. The effect of this may be to bias both product mix and refinery operating conditions toward those with relatively higher environmental costs. Even if this omission has no significant effect at Yorktown, it could be important at other refineries. Amoco acknowledges that the choice of feedstock may have a significant effect on environmental costs and is looking at this in more depth. The company might also examine the inputs and assumptions to both the Refinery Operating Plan and decisions on product mix to determine how much environmental costs vary with changing product mix.

To properly motivate refinery employees, the revised environmental costs should be reflected in incentive schemes, for top management at the refinery as well as for other employees. Financial performance targets should explicitly incorporate environmental considerations on the same footing as non-environmental ones. Programs like the Variable Incentive Plan, in which solid waste management currently constitutes 50 percent of the gain-sharing variable, should be extended to include other environmental activities that are consistent with the company's environmental goals and objectives.

The surprisingly large current cost of environmental activities, combined with the unknown but potentially sizable contingent liabilities, helps to explain Amoco's involvement in the regulatory process. This participation should focus on redirecting the process toward establishing environmental goals and reasonable phase-in schedules, rather than on mandating compliance methods.

Finally, Yorktown Refinery has demonstrated that it is possible to establish a cross-functional team to identify and quantify environmental costs. This team has made considerable progress toward integrating such information into normal refinery operations. A multilevel composition ensures that all levels in the company are represented, because each one has a unique task to perform in bringing a successful program on line. Amoco should now consider extending Yorktown's environmental accounting exercise to its other refineries. This would let it make comparisons of environmental performance, translated into cost terms, across all its refineries.

Notes

1. Amoco Corporation, Form 10-K, 1993.
2. Amoco Corporation, *Annual Report*, 1992.
3. American Petroleum Institute, *Petroleum Industry Environmental Performance*, Washington, D.C., 1992.

4. Letter to employees from William D. Ford, President, Amoco Oil Company, August 9, 1993.
5. William L. Leffler, *Petroleum Refining for the Nontechnical Person* (Tulsa, Okla.: Penn Well Publishing Company, 1985, 2nd ed.).
6. Amoco/U.S. Environmental Protection Agency (EPA), "Pollution Prevention Project Yorktown, Virginia: Project Summary," Revised, June 1992.
7. Amoco Oil Company, *Yorktown Refinery: Strategic Plan*, 1993.
8. Memo from K. Link to R. Farmer, P. Ward, and D. Hand, Amoco Oil Company, February 10, 1994.
9. J.J. McKetta (ed.), *Petroleum Processing Handbook* (New York: Marcel Dekker, Inc., 1992).
10. *International Petroleum Encyclopedia* (Tulsa, Okla.: Penn Well Publishing Company, 1992).
11. Memo from R.E. Schmitt to K. Link, Amoco Oil Company, June 15, 1994.
12. American Petroleum Institute, *Petroleum Industry Environmental Performance* (Washington, D.C.: 1993).
13. National Petroleum Council, *U.S. Petroleum Refining: Meeting Requirements for Cleaner Fuels and Refineries*, Executive Summary (Washington, D.C.: August 1993).
14. M. Porter, *Competitive Strategy: Techniques for Analyzing Industries and Competitors* (New York: Free Press, 1980); M. Porter, *Competitive Advantage: Creating and Sustaining Superior Performance* (New York: Free Press, 1985).
15. EPA, *Pollution Prevention Benefits Manual* (Washington, D.C.: October 1989).
16. Yorktown Refinery "Waste Minimization Accomplishments to Date," *Gain Sharing Committee News*, May 10, 1993.

III.
ENVIRONMENTAL ACCOUNTING CASE STUDY: CIBA-GEIGY

By Ajay Maindiratta and Rebecca Todd

1. Introduction

Ciba-Geigy Corporation is an internationally diversified company with headquarters in Basel, Switzerland. The company was formed in 1970 by the merger of CIBA and Geigy, both of which began as dyestuffs suppliers to the textile industry. Currently operating with 92,000 employees in 60 countries, Ciba is a major producer of pharmaceuticals, specialty chemicals, and agricultural products, diagnostic products, plant protection and animal health products, seeds, dyes, chemicals, additives, pigments, and polymers. The company's worldwide operations range from mature, low-growth products in the commodity chemicals divisions to higher growth specialty or niche chemicals, including value-added special formulations to meet individual customers' needs, to advanced technology-based high-growth pharmaceuticals. The company is vertically integrated, producing many of its own intermediate chemicals.

The Ciba corporate strategic policy statement defines three overall objectives: financial success, social responsibility, and environmental protection. The company seeks to remain or become market leader in each of its markets through sustainable growth. Reduction of energy consumption and waste in all forms are cited as company objectives. An internal environmental and safety audit is conducted periodically at all major sites.

This case study focuses on one product, *Stabilan*, a compound used to increase the shelf life and stability of a wide range of prod-

CASE HIGHLIGHTS: CIBA-GEIGY

This case study looks at an industrial chemical additive used to increase the shelf life and stability of a wide range of products. It is produced by Ciba-Geigy, a Swiss-based diversified company that is a major producer of pharmaceuticals, specialty chemicals, and agricultural products. The manufacturing process requires the use of several compounds that have significant environmental, health, or safety implications. One, a highly reactive substance, is a key building block in production of the intermediate; two solvents generate volatile organic compound emissions, and contribute to wastewater effluents.

Ciba-Geigy has a single, fully integrated general ledger system in use at all sites throughout the world. From the stand point of environmental costs, most traditional cost elements that can be quantified are currently recorded in some part of the accounting system. The authors conclude that a number of environmental costs are not variable, but fixed. A further important distinction is between out-of-pocket and historical costs; only the former can be reduced. However, for planning and control purposes, particularly in capital investment, historical cost items may signal important trends.

Many important environmental cost items cannot currently be determined from the accounts since the system does not explicitly separate them. To support decision-making and direct attention, the authors suggest that an "environmental profiling" of each product be done, with not only traditionally identified cost elements, such as wastewater treatment and solvent-recovery charges, but also with such less traditional costs as those for public relations for products with hazardous materials or effluent. The case study also identified environmental costs that could be expected to vary by manufacturing site in different countries.

—The editors

ucts. (*Stabilan* is a fictitious name for the product under study in this case.) The product is manufactured in the Additives Division of Ciba.

2. Market Context of the Additives Business and *Stabilan*

The Additives Division of Ciba produces natural and synthetic substances that are added in small amounts to a large number of materials to increase product life and quality. Additives are used as stabilizers for plastics, coatings, paints, color photographs, and lubricants.

Many of the products are specialty chemicals, high value-added products formulated to meet customer specifications regarding quality or delivery. These two factors directly affect customers' operations, both in the quality of the products and in production cost. Ciba has underlined the importance of quality as a key success factor for its divisions and sites by striving for ISO 9001 certification worldwide. This quality standard has already been granted to their Swiss and Italian facilities.

In addition, formulation of the product to meet each individual customer's process input specifications reduces or eliminates materials preprocessing stages in manufacturing and the resulting costs, including facilities, personnel, utilities, reactants, and wastes. Customers are willing to pay a small premium for such specially tailored products. Consequently, Ciba believes that another key success factor is the company's innovation and creativity in anticipating and meeting customers' needs, which not only secures the existing sales base but provides the potential for growth both in terms of unit sales and increased margins. The company regards this division as a core business with strong growth potential, especially in markets with particular needs for innovation, such as the coatings, graphics, photo, and electronics industries.

Stabilan is an additive used to improve the stability of plastic products. It is manufactured in both Europe and the United States, although domestic production is currently sold only in the U.S. market.

The product is manufactured on any of several flexible processing lines that have been constructed over the years and are used to produce other additives as well. Processing is done on a batch basis, with flushing of the lines between production runs. The principal material input for *Stabilan* is an intermediate produced in the same facility.

Research and development activities related to the product are conducted at the same site, with close cooperation between operating personnel and R&D staff. Committees consisting of operations and R&D staff meet periodically to consider proposals for product and process reformulations, including environmentally related projects, to assign priorities to such proposals, and to allocate necessary funds for R&D.

Continuing product and process reformulation for the Additives Division means that capital investment is made on a more or less continuing basis. The investments range from monitoring and control equipment to new processing facilities.

The organizational structure for the Additives Division follows the business structure. The closely related product group, manufactured in common facilities, is served by the same staff of employees including engineers, maintenance personnel, operators, accountants, environmental health and safety personnel, and managers. Additives Division managers are held accountable for profit and loss in the Division. Other services, such as legal, permitting, and waste treatment facilities, are supplied to the Division by joint facilities that serve other divisions as well. Because of the customer-driven nature of the additives business, marketing and manufacturing are very closely allied, and both short-term business and long-term strategic decision-making are centered in the division.

3. Environmental Context for *Stabilan*

3.1 Profile
This section briefly reviews the environmental dimensions of *Stabilan* with regard to both the product and the manufacturing processes used.

Because the product can be expected in normal use to come into contact with food, *Stabilan* must meet certain Food and Drug Administration guidelines, including toxicity safety testing required for comestible products. The product has been determined to be safe for human consumption as defined by those standards. Transportation and warehousing of *Stabilan* in its various formulations do not involve specific environmental hazards, such as elevated risk of inflammability, as defined by the insurance industry and state and local regulation. Currently, no state or local environmental permits or registrations are required, nor is the shipping or use of the product restricted.

The complex manufacturing process for *Stabilan* does require the use of several compounds that Ciba has identified as having significant environmental, health, or safety implications. One, a highly reactive substance, is a key building block in production of the intermediate; the other two, both solvents, lead to volatile organic compound (VOC) emissions as well as residues in wastewater effluents. As a consequence, these substances fall within the purview of a variety of federal, state, and local environmental regulations and are subject to permitting as well as rapidly proliferating governmental monitoring and reporting requirements. In addition, manufacturers are increasingly likely to be held responsible for the safe management of such effluents.

In light of increasingly stringent environmental regulation and the emerging legal liability environment, the company has committed to develop new processes for reclamation, reprocessing, and recycling of various emissions and effluents. In addition, managers and research staff have a goal of removing solvents and other highly reactive compounds from production as rapidly as process development will permit. This objective frequently involves major process redesign efforts. The ideal redesign from the company's point of view eliminates or reduces harmful substances while it increases production efficiency.

The division has had long-term R&D projects under way with the aim of reducing or removing altogether the use of certain compounds, removing purification processes through more efficient processing methods, and minimizing waste streams at the source (source reduction). These efforts have borne fruit in the case of a highly efficient new process that has eliminated solvents altogether. Similar efforts continue across the broad spectrum of the company's products. Such efforts frequently require basic research and are not only costly but can also involve lead times of a decade or more. R&D efforts for *Stabilan* are described by company personnel as being in a very early stage. However, the objective is ultimately to develop a process that requires neither highly reactive compounds nor solvents.

The manufacture of *Stabilan* produces wastewater streams as a result of production and flushing of lines for changeovers that must be processed at the on-site wastewater treatment facility. This plant receives manufacturing effluents as well as rainwater runoff and groundwater flows. The company plans to gradually reduce wastewater flows through improved waste recapture and recycling strategies in addition to improved manufacturing processes that reduce waste at the source. Since rainwater and groundwater flows will be processed for the foreseeable future, however, the water treatment plant is expected to be in use for the long term. As a consequence, the plant has been constructed in a manner that allows a portion of it to be shut down as waste flows are reduced. The company's current strategy is to develop waste treatment stages integral to individual manufacturing processes. As this objective is achieved, use of the central facilities can be expected to decline even further.

Ciba has a stated long-term goal of incinerating all organic waste streams. Alternatives external to the firm are under increasing regulatory pressure, and involve the assumption of potentially large contingency risks. Consequently, the company has built on-site incinerators at the manufacturing facility. However, Ciba wants to encourage the gradual reduction of incinerator usage by continual process development and improvement. At present, the wastewater treatment facility and the incinerators have excess operating capacity.

3.2 Environment-Driven Activities in the Additives Division
This section reports on the primary environment-driven activities associated with *Stabilan* with a view to determining where important decision support gaps may lie in the current management information system. The discussion is based on information elicited from Additives Division employees as well as service providers to the Division.

The Ciba managers regard R&D as essential to innovation and long-term manufacturing redesign. Additives R&D personnel estimate that at present as much as half of R&D expenditures may be driven by environment-related concerns. Decisions on initial development of project proposals, adoption of these proposals, and assignment of priorities to the projects are undertaken jointly by managers and R&D staff. Among the alternatives that managers may consider are:

1. directing significant efforts to long-term R&D projects for process redesign to remove solvents and highly reactive compounds, consistent with the company's long-term goals;
2. seeking to develop short- to-medium term improvements in solvent reclamation, recycling, and reprocessing in order to reduce wastewater effluents and VOC emissions; and
3. a combination of these approaches—that is, adopting short- to medium-term projects while pursuing long-term solutions.

The company engages in continuing capital replacement, improvement, and new investment—expenditures made to provide manufacturing capabilities not previously possessed by the division. Some capital investment projects are undertaken solely to comply with environmental regulations. Others achieve improvements in efficiency with attendant cost reductions while at the same time reducing waste. Capital investment proposals are developed internally in the division with discussion and support from corporate headquarters.

At a minimum, information support for R&D and capital investment decisions requires analysis of the total environmental cost of *Stabilan* in order to evaluate expected sacrifices and benefits associated with alternatives. The environmental cost elements should be sufficiently detailed to allow managers to determine which costs can be avoided under the alternatives.

Federal, state, and local regulatory compliance monitoring and reporting are an increasingly important function of the Additives Division engineering staff and managers. Employees report that these functions may take as much as 10–20 percent of normal working hours for some personnel, particularly engineers and managers, and that this number continues to increase. The time used for monitoring and reporting activities has grown rapidly in the last five years. As this happens, time available for process efficiency improvements and for creating new value-added specialty products and the like is reduced, an opportunity cost to the firm not measured by traditional accounting practice. Information support for monitoring and controlling these and similar environment-related costs requires not only details of environmental cost elements but also a sufficient number of periods to allow observation and tracking of emerging trends.

The company's policies and practice with regard to waste treatment are particularly important for both short- and long-term planning for the Additives Division and *Stabilan*. As the company has common wastewater treatment and incinerator facilities onsite, the related decisions faced by managers involve tradeoffs between waste facility usage, process redesign, and employee motivation in this decentralized organization.

Recharges (transfer prices) of joint services costs to the operating units that consume the services are made in order to achieve several objectives. In financial accounting for external reporting purposes, recharges are made to generate "full cost" Cost of Goods Sold and Inventory numbers. For managerial accounting, however, such recharges may be made to support a particular decision, such as determining the relevant costs of an investment alternative. Another common objective is to motivate employees to achieve a particular corporate objective. For example, if management wants to reduce waste generated by manufacturing units, one possible action is to charge waste treatment facility users either some "full cost" charge per unit for the services, or even an "overabsorbed" full cost charge, to penalize users and increase their incentive to pursue waste reduction strategies aggressively.

It should not be assumed automatically that a full cost charge is appropriate in all cases. Indeed, for a firm such as Ciba, which has corporate policies, accounting, and other procedures in place to foster long-term waste reduction at the source, the use of full cost recharges may have the undesired effect of encouraging managers to invest in short-term reclamation projects instead.

In other words, firms may use a variety of strategies to motivate managers to achieve corporate objectives, and product costing schemes are but one of them. Moreover, Ciba has excess capacity in the waste-treatment facilities at present. Thus, the company does not need to ration consumption of the resource in the near term.

For motivation and control purposes, management should carefully consider the company's objectives and the actions they wish managers to take; then they can formulate complementary waste treatment facility recharge rates and other contractual mechanisms to achieve these aims. The information support needed for these purposes would include variable and fixed out-of-pocket cost data as well as historical costs.

Legal, permitting, registration and contingent liability costs for *Stabilan* are very small at the present time and are not currently increasing, so the product does not raise significant issues in these areas. However, periodic monitoring on either a qualitative or a quantitative basis may be useful to detect important changes.

4. Description of the Ciba Accounting System

Ciba has developed a single, fully integrated general ledger system that is in use at all sites throughout the world. This means that the same data capture, analysis, aggregation, allocation, and reporting system is applied to operations in each company location. As legal, regulatory, and financial reporting practices as well as organizational structures differ from country to country, the system must be expanded to incorporate such inter-country differences. Thus, comparability of accounting data for operating results at different sites may be a direct function of the accounting and structural differences across countries. With regard to environmental costs, which are a function of differing legal, regulatory, and cultural attitudes toward the environment, substantial differences may be found in unit product full costs generated by the system.

The company's accounting system is quite comprehensive in initial data item recording. From the point of view of environmental costs, most traditional cost elements that can be quantified are currently recorded in some part of the accounting system. A list of strengths and weaknesses with regard to environmental cost identification and analysis is found in Table 6.

From a historical perspective, the sheer mass of such detailed information has led Ciba to form many cost pools which are then allocated according to various bases to specific divisions and eventually to products. Furthermore, because the company has a policy

Table 6. Strengths and Weaknesses of the Accounting System

Strengths
1. System is comprehensive—that is, designed to record all currently identified and estimable costs.
2. Allocation bases for some joint costs are subject to periodic review.
3. Corporate policy is to trace all costs, including environmental costs, to the products that produced them.
4. Managers have a good understanding of costs for which they are accountable.

Weaknesses
1. Economic nature of cost components (e.g., out-of-pocket/controllable or historical cost/noncontrollable) is not maintained in the aggregation and reporting process. Pooling mixes costs with varying degrees of controllability.
2. Allocation bases of cost pools do not, in general, distinguish between controllable and noncontrollable cost elements.
3. Short-term managerial decision-making based on pooled unit costs may be dysfunctional because of insufficient understanding of the nature of costs.
4. Production variances for joint units, such as the wastewater treatment facility, are routinely allocated back to all users at the end of the period, reducing individual managers' incentives to lower their use of the facilities by reducing wastewater flows.
5. As the full cost of joint services is allocated to users of the services, managers may find their own costs rising as other managers reduce consumption of the resource. Thus, managers are penalized for the efficiency of others. However, to the extent that such increased costs may provide incentives (higher opportunity costs) for the remaining managers to reduce waste, the process may not be wholly dysfunctional, provided that the company's long–term goals are not sacrificed in favor of short-term solutions.

of full product costing to the extent possible for managerial decision-making purposes, the detailed nature of many such environmental costs may be largely lost in the pooling and allocation process. That is, once an environmental cost item is added to a pool, it becomes part of the more generic overhead pool and the specific environmental attribute is lost for decision-making.

For example, some environmental costs, including R&D costs and depreciation on pollution control equipment, are added to common pools, including administrative cost for R&D and depreciation accounts for the equipment, and are then allocated without regard for the products that required or benefitted from the investments. In evaluating capital investments made to reduce pollution (and possibly increase yields)—for instance, investments that reduce flow or total organic carbon (TOC) to the wastewater treatment facility—Ciba does attempt to estimate savings. However, these are not always offset against the out-of-pocket (O-O-P) direct and indirect costs, which are reduced by the new investment. Thus managers' incentives to place high priority on identification and development of such opportunities may be substantially reduced.

Table 7 summarizes information from the *Stabilan* manufacturing cost sheets, focusing on the basic economic nature of cost items as direct, indirect, variable, fixed, and historical. During the on-site visit, the standard cost elements and supporting schedules were reviewed with accountants, with production supervisors and engineers, with environmental, health, and safety staff, and with waste treatment personnel to try to determine the economic nature of the line items as well as relevant environmental cost components, whether costs are currently identified as such or not.

At the request of Ciba, we have removed information on the cost of some important raw materials to safeguard potentially confidential data. As a consequence, all cost figures in this case study are expressed as a percentage of manufacturing costs excluding raw materials. These materials, which vary with and can be specifically identified with the product, are direct variable cost items. Allocations of historical costs for manufacturing equipment are labeled indirect historical costs in this context, as the equipment may be used to manufacture products other than *Stabilan*, and thus the costs must

93

Table 7. *Stabilan* Manufacturing Cost Analysis

Cost Component	O–O–P, DVC	O–O–P IVC	O–O–P IFC	HC
Raw Materials[1]		(see note below)		
Solvents	2			
Packaging Materials	2			
Materials Handling			<1	
Direct Labor			6	
Overhead			26	
Divisional Admin.			7	
Solvent Recovery			9	
Depreciation				13
Maintenance			8	
Electricity		3		<1
Steam		4	1	<1
Nitrogen			2	
Flow, TOC Charges		<1	4	<1
Analytical			2	
General Overhead			8	
Totals	4%	8%	74%	15%

1. Note: Raw materials costs are excluded from all calculations.

O–O–P = out–of–pocket
HC = historical costs
DVC = direct variable cost
IVC = indirect variable cost
IFC = indirect fixed cost

be allocated (rather than directly attributed) to the product. A number of costs are not variable but fixed. A further important distinction is between out-of-pocket and historical costs. Only the former, whether variable or fixed, can be reduced. However, for planning and control purposes, particularly in the case of capital investment, tracking of historical cost items may signal important trends.

A principal cost of *Stabilan* is an intermediate that is manufactured on-site as an input for a variety of different Ciba products. The transfer price used for the intermediate is a standard cost, partitioned into variable and fixed components. The cost elements for the intermediate have been decomposed and combined into the cost analysis scheme for *Stabilan*.

The identifiable out-of-pocket direct variable costs are limited to raw materials, solvents, and packaging materials. Out-of-pocket indirect variable costs were identified by studying individual facilities' cost sheets. The costs which are variable in nature (that is, increasing with volumes of production), but arise in joint facilities, are allocated back to consuming production units on a variety of bases. The bulk of costs, other than for materials, are out-of-pocket indirect fixed costs, and include labor and the largest portion of joint facilities costs.

It should be noted that "direct labor" is an indirect fixed cost, contrary to traditional treatment of labor as a variable cost. The direct labor force consists of operations technicians who are responsible for the production of several products in addition to *Stabilan*. Moreover, these personnel have not, in general, been subject to layoffs and rehirings but have been a stable pool. Thus, the cost of their labor does not rise and fall with production volumes. In addition, as these same technicians work on all the facility's products, the labor cost for *Stabilan* must be an allocated portion of the total "direct labor" cost and is labeled "indirect" as a consequence.

Overhead consists largely of managers' and supervisors' salaries. Administration is primarily ancillary services. "Solvent recovery" is an allocated indirect fixed cost for reclamation of a solvent used to produce *Stabilan*. Currently, capital expenditures for property, plant, and equipment are debited to plant and equipment accounts without distinguishing between expenditures made for general process improvements and those made expressly for environmental reasons, whether voluntary or to comply with regulations. Thus, it is not possible, at present, to develop information regarding the relative magnitudes of such costs or their rate of growth in recent years.

Maintenance is similar to the labor and overhead costs in that a pool of personnel work on all of the facilities that produce *Stabilan* as well as the other products. Electricity, steam, and nitrogen charges are reallocations of joint costs or joint facilities costs. "Flow, TOC charges" are, respectively, costs for the volume of wastewater flow and dissolved total organic carbon in the water sent to the wastewater treatment facility. These are based on engineering estimates. "Analytical" is an allocation to *Stabilan* for production quality control testing. General overhead is the headquarters cost reallocated to the product.

Each of the cost components listed in the schedule may have some environmental implication. But the specific environmental attribute of the line items varies widely. Solvent costs are slightly less than 2 percent of the total, excluding raw materials. Indirect variable costs identified in the analysis are approximately 8 percent, a relatively small proportion. Indirect out-of-pocket fixed costs are about three-quarters of the manufacturing costs, again excluding raw materials. The identified depreciation charges from all sources are about 15 percent of this total.

This analysis finds that more than 85 percent of the identified cost of *Stabilan* (excluding materials) is for environmentally related out-of-pocket costs—for example, personnel and other costs (including time spent on environmental regulatory compliance and monitoring, process testing and control, and R&D, as well as similar costs for materials recovery and recycling and waste treatment. This implies that they are susceptible to company environmental cost reduction efforts.

Table 8 provides a summary of "environmental" cost items for *Stabilan*. This list takes a very broad view of environmental relevance, flagging all items described as having some environmental implications. Those that are clearly separable are the costs of wastewater treatment and solvent recovery, which together account for approximately 15 percent of the total manufacturing costs of *Stabilan* (excluding raw materials). Given the current Ciba accounting system, it is not possible to estimate an upper or lower bound for the environmental proportion of a number of cost elements. Rather than set arbitrary bounds, we have used theoretical limits. Clearly, the lower bound understates and the upper bound

Table 8. *Stabilan* Environmental Cost Analysis

Cost Component	Estimated Environmental Portion (%)	Environmental Cost as a Percentage of Total
Raw Materials[1]	(see note below)	
Solvents	0 – 100	0 – 2
Packaging Materials	0 – 100	0 – 2
Materials Handling	0 – 100	<1
Direct Labor	3	<1
Overhead	10 – 25	3 – 7
Divisional Administration	0 – 100	0 – 7
Solvent Recovery	100	9
Depreciation	0 – 100	0 – 13
Maintenance	0 – 100	0 – 8
Electricity	10 – 80	<1 – 3
Steam	20 – 80	1 – 4
Nitrogen	20 – 80	<1 – 2
Flow, TOC Charges	100	6
Analytical	0 – 100	0 – 2
General Overhead	0 – 100	0 – 8
Totals		19% – 72%

1. *Note:* Raw materials costs are excluded from all calculations.

substantially overstates the environmental costs. For example, in no case would we expect the environmental proportion of administrative costs to be as high as 100 percent. Among our recommendations is the proposal that Ciba managers consider further analysis and refinement of these bounds to enhance the quality of environmental information available to managers.

R&D costs do not appear in this schedule because development efforts for *Stabilan* are currently in a very early stage. In fact, R&D

costs would not normally be a part of manufacturing cost schedules under traditional systems based on financial reporting. Nonetheless, discussion with R&D personnel at Ciba reveals that such costs are frequently driven at least in part, if not entirely, by environmental concerns and would be relevant cost items for some managerial decisions regarding the environment. Ciba currently incorporates such expenditures into divisional cost statements as a component of administrative overhead cost pools.

One of the potentially largest environmental cost items for *Stabilan* is the time spent by managers, engineers, and technicians on environmental training, monitoring, and compliance, along with managers' strategy, policy, and planning time and efforts. For example, engineers estimate that they spend 176 hours a year on regulatory reporting activities, 400 hours on waste shipment processing, 600 hours on sampling and analysis, and 300 hours on environmental monitoring, for an annual total of some 1,476 hours.

By all accounts, during the last five years, managers are doing more on environmental activities and this may take up to 25 percent or more of their time. Table 8 reports estimated ranges for environmental personnel costs based on discussions with employees. Such environmental efforts, although essential, represent an increasing opportunity cost to the firm. That is, as more time is devoted to environmental issues, less is available for cost reduction efforts and other planning activities. Moreover, environmental activities must receive highest priority, as the division's ability to continue is contingent on regulatory compliance. Obviously, the firm could, at additional cost, hire more managers, engineers, and other employees. Although the personnel time constraint is nonbinding and may be eased by means of additional expenditures, the regulatory constraints are absolutely binding.

Many important environmental cost items cannot currently be determined from the accounts as the system does not explicitly separate them. For example, expenditures for pollution control devices are grouped with other capital expenditure items and appear only as a portion of allocated depreciation. The company maintains a policy of "full cost allocation," but the economic nature of many of the costs, including environmental ones, is lost in the aggregation process.

5. Recommendations

5.1 Environmental Managerial Accounting Changes

The current Ciba accounting system is primarily designed to produce financial accounting and reporting information rather than managerial decision information. Thus, cost items are largely historical in nature. The current traditional reporting formats are segmented along manufacturing, marketing, and headquarters cost categories. Many important environmental costs are dispersed throughout the reporting system. For example, although solvent recovery costs are charged back, anticipated R&D costs to remove solvents from the manufacturing process altogether will appear as a divisional cost element, disassociated from the manufacturing process that will eventually benefit. Moreover, as environmental concerns are an integral part of Ciba's business philosophy, the company sees little practical value in capturing every possible environmental component included in the various cost elements.

Ciba seeks "win-win" operational improvements—that is, changes that eliminate environmental wastes while reducing costs as well. For example, if a particular solvent, subject to regulatory oversight, is removed, then costs are reduced not only for materials but also for regulatory monitoring and reporting, wastewater treatment, toxic materials handling, maintenance and monitoring of reclamation and recycling equipment and related utilities costs, and possibly a host of others as well.

To evaluate the costs and benefits of such improvements, Ciba should explore the possibility of expanding the current system to produce schedules specifically designed for disclosure of relevant costs for particular decisions. Most of the information is presently known or obtainable at relatively low cost by company managers and staff. In many cases, all that is needed is an additional account indicator code at the time materials are purchased, capital expenditures are made, and labor activities are initially reported. For example, an R&D manager indicates that estimates of environment-related cost elements for R&D projects can usually be made with reasonable accuracy at project completion. As managers and R&D staff have defined project objectives before projects are undertaken, it is likely that more timely estimations of the relevant environmental cost components may be possible as costs are incurred, along the lines of conventional accounting practice for long-term construction projects. Evaluation of "hidden" costs (personnel, monitoring, etc.) may be relevant for assigning priorities to alternative R&D projects and for decisions on potential capital expenditures for automated monitoring and control equipment. In cases where precise estimation is not possible, qualitative data—such as unpartioned totals—possibly accompanied by ranges of proportions, may prove useful in sensitivity analysis and in determining whether costs are "material."

To support attention-directing and decision-making, an "environmental profiling" of each product could be done along the lines of Table 8. The profile should incorporate not only traditionally identified cost elements, such as wastewater treatment and solvent recovery charges, but also the full range of environmental activities, including less traditional costs such as public relations for products with hazardous materials or effluents.

Second, careful consideration should be given to the reasons for manufacturing service facility recharges to the divisions consuming some portion of those resources. Specifically, management should examine the motivational implications of such recharges, ensuring that the corporate goals, such as for the reduction of environmental waste, are indeed being furthered by these charges. As we have observed, the recharge system and distribution of variances or residuals at the end of the period may have the undesired effect of lowering managers' incentives to reduce waste because their divisions will not see the immediate direct benefit of the reduction.

Environmental and other manufacturing costs, including contingent liability exposure, tend to follow technologies. Thus, to better monitor and control technology-driven costs, some managerial accounting reports should be segmented along the lines of major technologies. To some extent this is already being done in the *Stabilan* facility cost reports, because the same unit manufactures an intermediate as well as several products that use the compound as a major input. Ciba should first identify important common technologies that may be used in different market product groups, where accounting may follow marketing lines rather than technologies. Then, an evaluation of cost-drivers specific to individual technologies may provide insight into additional opportunities for cost reduction.

5.2 International Manufacturing Cost Comparisons
Proposals for an initial revised cost schedule for international manufacturing cost comparisons are presented in Table 9. The first section includes line items that are most nearly comparable between countries and sites—materials costs. To the extent processes differ, of course, line items will be more or less comparable.

Table 9. Proposed *Stabilan* Manufacturing Cost Reformulation for Inter–Site Comparisons

I.   Direct Out–of–Pocket
     Raw Materials
     Solvents
     Packaging Materials

II. Recharged Manufacturing Services
     Materials Handling
     Direct Labor
     Solvent Recovery
     Maintenance
     Electricity
     Steam
     Nitrogen
     Wastewater Treatment
     Analytical

III. Allocated Manufacturing Overhead
     Depreciation
     Overhead
     Administration
     General Overhead

The second section lists recharges of joint manufacturing services that are required for manufacturing. Since individual variable out-of-pocket and historical cost elements are relatively small, they have been merged with the fixed out-of-pocket costs. Recharges are a function of many economic factors, including age of facilities, technology employed, and volume of usage. Thus, comparisons here are more problematic.

The final category includes managerial, supervisory, and other overhead costs as well as corporate overhead recharges. Such costs are a function of organizational structure and scope of products produced in a division, and are difficult to compare.

The focus in any comparisons must be on "escapability" from the point of view of the corporation, rather than simply the individual product. For example, if a certain level of cost will continue whether or not *Stabilan* is manufactured, then it is not relevant for international manufacturing cost comparisons. It is entirely possible that the majority of joint manufacturing services costs in the plant facility may decline only slightly, if at all, if the manufacture of *Stabilan* were discontinued at that site.

6. Conclusions

Ciba-Geigy may benefit by expanding the scope of the current managerial accounting system to permit increased detail in recording individual data items (especially with regard to environmental costs) and to consider the potential usefulness to decision-makers of more flexible cost-reporting formats, focusing for each major decision category on the relevant costs.

The recommendations for changes to the managerial accounting system and international manufacturing cost analysis differ in some respects because the managerial decision context differs. Consequently, the relevant costs vary. In the first case, managers need to know the total cost burden to the company as a whole for *Stabilan* production. Consequently, the opportunity costs of managers' time and effort—time that could be spent on other activities (for example, cost reduction) but must be devoted to regulatory compliance and monitoring efforts—are relevant. For international cost comparisons, however, as only a small portion of such costs can be avoided in the short term, the costs are unlikely to be materially relevant.

The recommendations of this case study are essentially for enhancements to fine-tune the existing system, as Ciba has already taken initial steps in some of the areas. The basic suggestion is to add dimensions to the system that better reflect the actual operating and decision-making aspects of the business.

IV.
ENVIRONMENTAL ACCOUNTING CASE STUDY: DOW CHEMICAL

By Ajay Maindiratta and Rebecca Todd

1. Introduction

The Dow Chemical Company, an internationally diversified firm, is the second largest chemical company in the United States, with worldwide sales of more than $18 billion.[1] Historically, the chemical industry has been highly competitive and cyclical—that is, very sensitive to changing economic conditions. Dow Chemical produces more than 2,000 products and services, with no single product accounting for more than 5 percent of sales.

The company was organized in Michigan in 1897 to extract chemicals from the native brine deposits in the central part of the state. Since then, it has expanded from bromine and chloralkali into chlorinated organics, phenolics, and a variety of bulk and specialty chemicals. Dow Chemical has organized operations along matrix lines for some time. Recently, the company has been changing to a more streamlined matrix hierarchy, two dimensions of which are geographical region and business group. The latter category includes Chemicals and Performance Products, Plastics, and Hydrocarbons and Energy as well as other business functions.

Dow Chemical is vertically integrated and produces a variety of intermediate products used as inputs to the manufacture or processing of customer products. The markets for these products include the chemical processing, pulp and paper, personal care, pharmaceutical, processed foods, and utility industries. In addition to the industry segments, Dow Chemical has formed several

CASE HIGHLIGHTS: DOW CHEMICAL

This case study looks at a polymer-based coating material made by Dow Chemical, the second largest U.S. chemical company. In manufacturing this product, significant quantities of two volatile organic compounds are released. Corporate commitments to reduce wastes, together with pending regulations under the Clean Air Act, require major changes to curtail emissions if the plant is to remain open. The authors review Dow's environmental cost accounting practices and relate these to the decision to upgrade or abandon this unit. The case also touches on environmental cost with a view to product portfolio and pricing decisions.

The company has a single, fully integrated general ledger system designed to provide a traditional "full product costing" of manufacturing services, facilities, and corporate overhead to manufacturing plants and divisions. Most traditional environmental costs that can be quantified are currently recorded in some part of the system.

In analyzing the standard cost information for the product, the authors found that 3.2 percent of the total manufacturing cost fell in the conventional "environmental" category—waste disposal and treatment. The environment-related components of such items as operating labor, managers' salaries, and planning efforts are not distinguished as environmental. Nor are the environmentally relevant portions of capital investment, represented by depreciation allocations, as provided by the manufacturing cost sheets.

The authors categorized costs according to their economic nature: variable, fixed, direct, indirect, out-of-pocket, and historical. Those with potential environmental significance are predominantly fixed. If the plant were closed, the only costs the company as a whole would escape are the out-of-pocket direct and indirect variable costs.

—The editors

operating partnerships and ventures with other firms including Dow Corning, DowElanco, and Marion Merrell Dow.

The company has had comprehensive environmental policies in place for a long time. Its policy is:

> to prevent pollution through excellence in plant design and operation. Waste generated is recycled whenever possible. When waste is treated, off-site disposal has been minimized by operating incinerators, biological treatment plants, and landfills on company property. Costs of site remediation are accrued as a part of the shutdown costs of a facility. The nature of such remediation could include cleanup of soil contamination or the closure of landfills and waste treatment ponds.[2]

Dow Chemical regards pollution as an indicator of process inefficiency, a view that can be traced back at least three decades. For example, David Buzzelli, Vice President and Corporate Director of Environment, Health & Safety, observed, "Carl Gerstacker, our chairman in the mid-1960s, emphasized that pollution was basically a loss of yield.... More emissions meant loss of valuable resources. So we began looking at ways to improve process efficiencies and reduce wastes."[3] In addition, the company has a long-standing policy of investing in on-site treatment facilities, a practice that they maintain accounts for their low Superfund liabilities relative to other major chemical producers.

This case study focuses on a polymer-based coating material produced at a single facility by the Specialty Polymer and Intermediates Division. *Duragen* is a fictitious name for the product under study in this case.

2. Market Context of the *Duragen* Business

Duragen is a polymer-based product that has particular film strength and solubility properties useful for a variety of purposes, including as a viscosity modifier and a coating agent. It has been produced by Dow Chemical for many years and is considered a mature product; that is, the market's capacity to absorb large increases in sales volume is expected to be limited. Yet, the product has a number of uses that provide a relatively stable market for *Duragen* for the foreseeable future. Its market price was not increased for approximately a decade. Recently, customers have accepted modest price increases, although competition for the product does exist. Part of this may be due to customer servicing policies for this product: the company strives to meet customers' quality specifications and other requirements.

3. Environmental Context for *Duragen*

3.1 Profile
The *Duragen* plant is one of several hundred production units at the manufacturing site. The plant and processes for *Duragen* have been in place for better than 20 years, with the exception of a new tank farm facility constructed in the last decade in response to environmental regulations. The main ingredients of *Duragen* are reacted and the resulting mixture is then purified, dewatered, and dried.

The current manufacturing operations are not particularly efficient, and substantial amounts of waste effluents are produced in processing *Duragen*. At present, roughly six pounds of raw materials are consumed in the production of one pound of *Duragen*. The process results in the release of a variety of air emissions, including two volatile organic compounds (VOCs). A significant proportion of the manufacturing process is devoted to recovery of these potential air pollutants. Even so, a substantial quantity of VOCs is released to the atmosphere.

In addition, the manufacturing process generates liquid waste that is sent to a shared on-site wastewater treatment plant and solid wastes that are incinerated or landfilled. Waste generation varies with the grade of the product. Generally, higher grade products generate greater quantities of air pollution and waste water.

Many major business decisions revolve around capital investment; for example, the company conducted capital investment analyses for the new tank farm investment in the late 1980s. It had to invest or shut down because of new environmental regulations on underground storage tanks. The regulatory constraint was binding in that case and, according to the managers and analysts familiar with the decision-making, the analysis was performed on an ad hoc basis.

The company has recently established an internal economic analysis group tasked, among other things, with preparing comprehensive economic analyses (including, for example, discounted cash flow modeling) of capital investment proposals for feasibility review. Currently, all capital investment proposals above $2 million receive extensive reviews at various levels of the company's chain of command.

The *Duragen* plant is again faced with major operating changes, including possible new capital expenditures, in order to meet regulatory requirements of the Clean Air Act that become effective in 1997, as well as emissions eliminations under the Environmental Protection Agency's 33/50 voluntary reductions plan. Release of two VOCs during the production of *Duragen* will no longer be permitted. The company thus faces investing in new technology for substantial reduction of emissions or eventual shutdown. The needed technology currently exists, although it is expected to cost $3 million.

Operating and marketing managers state that customers for *Duragen* have been receptive to price increases, in part because marketing personnel have explained that the increases are required to meet new environmental requirements and the associated capital investments.

3.2 Environment-Driven Activities Related to Duragen Manufacture

The decisions that Dow Chemical must make depend on the product's operating and environmental context and environment-driven activities. The regulatory constraints resulting from the VOC emissions under the Clean Air Act are binding—the company cannot, by its own operating initiatives, eliminate this constraint. The decision to make the capital investment in new technology is thus an economic one based on the product's expected future profitability and viability.

Managers rely on management accounting systems for three somewhat related reasons: for support in making decisions on operating and capital budgeting alternatives; for monitoring, in order to take advantage of opportunities to improve operational efficiency or to achieve other economic benefits; and for control of ongoing operations and as motivation for employees to achieve corporate goals.

Accounting information, including environmental information, is costly to produce, and its benefit is measured by the relative value of the information in making a particular decision. If, for example, a manager does not find an item of accounting information either relevant or useful for a particular decision, then its value to him is zero. As all business decisions are necessarily context-dependent—the specific information items that are useful will vary depending upon the decision to be made. In this sense, management accounting information systems differ considerably from financial reporting systems. Thus although a firm will produce a single schedule of revenues and expenses (a net income statement) for external reporting, it may provide a wide variety of different cost and/or income schedules to decision-makers, depending on their managerial information needs.

First, the company desires a general review of its environmental cost accounting practices. As this is necessarily a subset of the larger management accounting system, the task entails a broader review of the entire system. Second, the plant managers wish to review cost accounting practice for *Duragen* with an eye to the forthcoming capital budgeting decision. This study does not focus on the capital budgeting process itself—the economic analysis unit has conducted reviews of the expected expenditures—but rather on the relevant manufacturing costs for *Duragen* in the context of this decision.

The *Duragen* plant produces many grades of the product plus two by-products, for which there is an outside market. If only a single product were produced, the plant's capacity (in pounds) would vary substantially and the margins on the different products would vary as well. However, at present the plant is not operating at capacity and there are consequently no binding capacity constraints. Nonetheless, a third reason for the analysis is to review the current costing practice with a view to the *Duragen* plant's product portfolio and pricing decisions. That is, the managers may find that changes can be made, either in the mix of products offered or in the prices of one or more of the products, that would enhance the plant's, and consequently the company's, overall profitability.

Thus, the case study review of the company's environmental and management accounting practice focuses on the following questions:

1. Are the costs of environmental activities identified by the management accounting system, and is the economic nature of such costs preserved through the aggregation process for managerial decision-making?
2. Which of the product's manufacturing costs and which of the company's (i.e., outside of the *Duragen* plant) manufacturing services and other overhead costs recharged to *Duragen* are relevant to the decision on investing or shutting down?
3. Which costs are relevant to *Duragen* product portfolio and pricing decisions?

4. Description of the Accounting System

The company has developed a single, fully integrated general ledger system that is designed to provide a traditional "full product costing" of manufacturing services facilities and other corporate overhead to manufacturing plants and divisions. The process at Dow Chemical follows a conventional pattern. Costs are collected at cost centers (e.g., individual manufacturing lines), then successively aggregated upward through plants, geographical sites, legal entities, regions, and, ultimately, the fully consolidated entity—the Dow Chemical Company.

The company's system is relatively comprehensive in initial data item recording. From the point of view of environmental costs, most traditional costs that can be quantified are currently recorded in some part of the accounting system. Some strengths and weaknesses of the accounting system with regard to identification and analysis of environmental costs are given in Table 10.

Over the years, Dow Chemical has developed an extensive infrastructure of interlocking manufacturing services facilities, in-

Table 10. Strengths and Weaknesses of the Accounting System

Strengths

1. System is comprehensive—i.e., designed to capture all traditional identifiable and estimable costs.
2. Corporate policy is to trace all costs, including identified environmental costs, to the products that produced them.
3. Most pooling is done at the individual facility level (e.g., incineration) rather than at higher organizational levels.
4. Managers have a good understanding of costs for which they are responsible.

Weaknesses

1. Economic nature of cost components (e.g., out-of-pocket/controllable or historical cost/non-controllable) is not maintained in the aggregation and reporting process. Economically different costs are pooled, mixing costs of varying degrees of controllability. Allocation bases of cost pools do not distinguish between controllable and non-controllable cost elements.
2. Short-term managerial decision-making based on pooled unit costs may be dysfunctional because of insufficient understanding of the nature of the costs.
3. As the full cost (marginal) of joint services is allocated to users of the services, managers may find their own costs rising as other managers reduce consumption of the resource. Thus, some managers are penalized for the efficiency of others. However, to the extent that such increased costs may provide incentives (higher opportunity costs) for the remaining managers to reduce waste, the process may not be wholly dysfunctional.
4. Managers in manufacturing divisions will tend to regard the recharges as "variable" costs when in fact large portions may be inescapable fixed or historical.

cluding maintenance, purchasing, technical services, engineering, wastewater treatment, incineration, and solid waste disposal. These facilities and activities in general provide services to all product manufacturing divisions and plants. In order to provide "full manufacturing costs" as required by conventional financial reporting practices, the costs of operations of the joint facilities are recharged to the manufacturing units on a variety of recharge or allocation bases, such as volumes of wastewater produced and hours of "normal" or "priority" maintenance.

The costs—whether out-of-pocket (O-O-P) variable, out-of-pocket fixed, or historical (e.g., depreciation and amortization)—are allocated for the most part on a single basis. That is, the operating costs for a joint facility are pooled, regardless of the economic nature of the cost, and the aggregated costs are then distributed among users on the recharge basis. Thus, distinctions according to the economic nature of the costs are lost in the recharge process. Such simplifications of accounting allocation have developed historically from the sheer mass of detailed information that must be recharged for financial full costing purposes from largely manual general ledger operations. With modern computer operations, however, cost/benefit constraints on accounting data recording and allocation are no longer binding.

Another implication of the company's recharge system is that to the extent that decision-relevant environmental items are dispersed throughout the various service facilities, important information may be lost in the pooling and allocation process. Once an environmental cost item is added to a pool, it becomes part of the more generic overhead pool and the specific environmental attribute is lost for decision-making. For example, to the extent that maintenance or R&D activities are conducted for environmental purposes, information will be lost if the specific purpose of the activity is not preserved in the system. As a result, it is not uncommon to find that a portion of the cost of environment-related activities is hidden in personnel costs, salaries, and wages.

Owing to the considerable strengths of the current system in terms of initial data capture, the primary changes that the company might contemplate are modifications that will permit the environmental and economic nature of the costs to be retained in the aggregation and management reporting process, so that such costs can be specifically identified in the managers' decision-making processes. (Implications of the system for both the plant's and the company's management decisions are discussed in later sections.)

Some environmental costs, including capital expenditures for pollution-control equipment, are added to common pools (such as generic plant or divisional property, plant, and equipment accounts), and the environmental attribute is lost. Depreciation is recorded as a single generic line item and the opportunity cost of capital expended for environmental purposes is lost. Capital investments made to reduce pollution (and possibly increase yields)—for example, investments that reduce flow or solids to the wastewater treatment facility—are not offset against O-O-P direct and indirect costs reduced by the new investment. Thus, managers' incentives to place high priority on identification and development of such opportunities are substantially reduced.

Table 11 summarizes the *Duragen* manufacturing standard cost sheets, focusing on the basic economic nature of cost items as direct, indirect, variable, fixed, and historical to the extent that the current costing system will permit. For example, raw materials, which vary with and can be specifically identified with a product, are variable cost items. Allocations of depreciation for manufacturing equipment are labeled indirect historical costs in this context, as the equipment may be used to manufacture other products as well, and thus the costs must be allocated to *Duragen*. A number of costs—for example, labor costs of manufacturing—are not variable in the conventional accounting sense but fixed, as the company recognizes them. This is because labor is not subject to layoffs, except in the case of plant closings and consolidations. It is also important to distinguish between out-of-pocket and historical costs. Only the former can be reduced.

The proportions used here are standard costs based upon budgets. *Duragen* High Grade was selected for this illustration because it is one of the highest-volume products during the period studied. Moreover, the yield is relatively high and the costs are in the middle range, compared with other *Duragen* products. Thus, it is reasonably representative of the plant's production costs.

Table 11. *Duragen* Manufacturing Cost Analysis

Cost Component	E	O-O-P DVC%	O-O-P IVC%	O-O-P IFC%	HC%
Other Raw Materials		21.0			
Solvent	*	1.0			
Proprietary Reactant	*	14.9			
By–Products		–3.0			
Packaging Materials		2.8			
Wastewater Treatment	*	1.8			
Operating Labor				14.8	
Maintenance Charges				10.9	
Utilities			9.4	3.3	
Packaging Materials				<0.1	
Supplies				1.8	
Research & Development				1.3	
Other Recharges				4.2	
Water Waste	*			0.6	
Solids (Wastewater)	*			0.1	
Rubbish to Pit	*			0.2	
Incinerator (liquids)	*			<0.1	
Incinerator (solids)	*			0.1	
Non–hazardous Landfill	*			<0.1	
Depreciation	*				5.7
Taxes & Insurance				2.3	
Factory Expenses			<0.1	5.9	
Other Cost				0.3	
Total Manufacturing Cost		**39.0**	**9.5**	**45.9**	**5.7**

As can be seen from the Table, direct variable costs—primarily for raw materials—account for approximately 39 percent of the total manufacturing cost. The indirect variable costs, mainly variable utility recharges, are approximately 10 percent of the total. Thus about half the costs, as indicated in the company's costing

115

system, are variable. About 46 percent of the total is reallocations or recharges of joint (or common) facilities costs, of which only a small portion is directly charged to the plant. The remaining costs are depreciation allocations.

An investigation of the relative proportions of out-of-pocket variable and fixed costs for three of the joint facilities (incinerator, wastewater treatment, and landfill) revealed the following: 44 percent of the incinerator costs are out-of-pocket variable and an additional 15 percent are out-of-pocket fixed; for the wastewater treatment facility, the proportions are 49 percent and 28 percent, respectively; and for the landfill, 95 percent of the costs are out-of-pocket fixed. The implication is that the economic interpretation of the various recharge numbers can vary considerably, depending on the relative "escapability" of the charges. Recall that only out-of-pocket charges are susceptible to control, and only the variable portion can be controlled in the short run. Historical cost allocations (e.g., depreciation) are not useful for current decision-making except to the extent that they are reasonable proxies for the opportunity costs of capital.

Costs with some environmental attribute are indicated with an asterisk in Table 11 and summarized in Table 12. Conventional "environmental" costs that focus on waste disposal and treatment represent about 3.2 percent of the total. No cost was included for the time non-environmental labor devote to environmental activities. The rationale of the plant manager was that attention to environmental issues was an inescapable aspect of every employees' job. The environmentally relevant portions of capital investment, represented by depreciation allocations, are not routinely segregated in the manufacturing cost sheets, but were estimated to be in the range of zero to ten percent of the total depreciation allocation.

The precise nature of the environmental attribute varies among items. For example, the solvent and the proprietary reactant account for approximately 16 percent of the entire product cost of *Duragen* High Grade, and better than one-third of the direct variable costs. The residuals of these materials must be recaptured from effluent streams to the extent economically feasible. Recapture represents recovery of product cost (less cost of recapture); waste treatment of residuals represents lost product and inefficient

Table 12. Summary of Environmental Costs for *Duragen*

Cost Item	Estimated Environmental Percentage	Environmental Cost as a Percentage of Total
Wastewater treatment	100	2.2
Water Waste	100	0.6
Solids (Wastewater)	100	0.1
Rubbish to Pit	100	0.2
Incinerator (liquids)	100	<0.1
Incinerator (solids)	100	0.1
Non–hazardous Landfill	100	<0.1
Depreciation	0 – 10	0 – 0.6
Totals		3.2 – 3.8

Other Potentially Relevant Costs:

Solvent	0 – 100	0 – 1.0
Proprietary Reactant	0 – 100	0 – 14.9
Maintenance	0 – 100	0 – 10.9
R&D	0 – 100	0 – 1.3

use of resources. However, these residuals vary substantially across the grades of *Duragen*.

Maintenance and R&D charges frequently include some environmentally relevant portions. Consequently, they have been included in Table 12 even though they do not at present have environmental significance in the case of *Duragen*. If the costs of the solvent and the proprietary reactant are included (as some portion must either be recovered or treated), the environmental costs may range up to approximately 20 percent.

A particular problem illustrated in this analysis is that traditional costing practice, which reflects only past (historical) incurred costs, may severely underestimate environmental cost ex-

posure. For example, the solvent represents only about one percent of the total product cost of *Duragen*. Yet, use of the solvent
and a proprietary reactant, both of which release VOCs, has compelled management to consider a major capital investment in
order to comply with provisions of both the Clean Air Act and the
33/50 program. The alternative is to cease operations altogether.
Thus, although historical cost of the solvent is minuscule, and it is
unlikely that its size would trigger a management decision to replace the solvent, the resulting environmental cost exposure is
very large. Moreover, traditional costing practice will not link the
two.

One of the most serious difficulties with the current reporting
system is that managers cannot clearly distinguish on an ongoing
basis the effects of potential decisions such as discontinuing operations in a particular manufacturing plant or division based on the
data available in the manufacturing cost sheets.

As indicated, the variable out-of-pocket portion of many joint
costs, the only "escapable" part in the short run, is perhaps only
half of the joint costs recharged. If the plant should cease operations, then about half of the joint allocated costs would still be incurred. Thus, only 71 percent of the *Duragen* cost could be escaped
and is relevant to a shutdown decision in this hypothetical example. Yet, the exact share is unknown and unknowable from the current cost reporting system. The numbers are likely to be material to
business decisions in any case.

A second problem is that the full costing recharge process,
which is designed for financial reporting rather than management
decision-making, does not address the issue of behavior motivation of managers in order to achieve the company's strategic goals.
The company has long stated its corporate commitment to reduce
waste and to streamline operations in order to improve competitiveness. Thus, corporate attention should be given to why the joint
services recharges are being made to the divisions for internal
managerial decision-making. Indeed, plant managers are constrained to a great extent in their efforts to reduce wastewater and
other effluents and wastes by the efficiency of the manufacturing
plant currently in place. A "win-win" solution could be based on a
decision to trade off new capital expenditures to improve process

efficiency against such costs as variable water treatment costs, solids incineration, and other such escapable costs under the new process.

As noted, the obvious environmental costs, such as waste treatment costs, are apparently readily identifiable in the cost schedules. (We do not deal here with the proliferation of such recharges throughout the system to the various facilities, which then recharge these back to manufacturing divisions.) Additional environmental activity costs are likely to be "hidden" in other charges. These costs cannot be identified in the current costing process. Many of them, including legal costs, product registration and fees, and public relations costs for products involving hazardous materials, occur outside of the usual manufacturing site and normally only reach the manufacturing level in the form of corporate overhead allocations to manufacturing profit and loss schedules, but not identified with the products giving rise to them.

5. Recommendations

5.1 Revisions to the Environmental Cost Accounting System

Given the company's stated policy of identifying the costs of environmental and other wastes that represent lost yields and profitability, Dow Chemical should consider "environmental profiling" of its various activities with environmental attributes. For example, the costs of manual environmental monitoring and regulatory reporting could be lowered through less costly automated operations and devices. Managerial time spent on such activities may be consolidated or otherwise delegated to achieve efficiencies.

Such "profiling" will necessarily involve some double counting to the extent that some activities have, for example, both environmental and profit-improving aspects. This is not a problem for managerial decision-making because managers, with expert knowledge of their operations, can make the necessary qualitative judgements to weight the items. Moreover, these numbers are not being "summed" for conventional financial reporting purposes in this instance. Clearly, such decision-oriented data partitioning and scheduling could be applied to other non-environmental decisions as well.

5.2 The Plant's Capital Investment Decision

As noted earlier, the only costs the company as a whole will escape if *Duragen* ceases production are the out-of-pocket direct and indirect variable costs resulting from production. Out-of-pocket indirect fixed and all historical costs are not relevant to the decision. A review of the costs in Table 11 suggests that the direct variable costs (39 percent of the total), the indirect variable utility costs (9.5 percent), the indirect fixed labor charges (14.8 percent), and an undeterminable proportion of the remaining indirect fixed charges are out-of-pocket escapable charges that will cease with shutdown. Any portion of the "indirect fixed" common charges that is out-of-pocket will be borne by other users of the facilities under the current accounting system practice. But in fact they are ultimately the responsibility of the company as a whole. Historical cost allocations, unless viewed as opportunity costs of capital, are distributions of "sunk" costs—that is, past expenditures that are not relevant to these decisions.

For internal managerial decision-making, Dow Chemical may wish to consider the desirability of hierarchical statements that retain costs, such as the out-of-pocket fixed costs of common facilities, at higher corporate levels—at least for some important corporate decisions, including most capital budgeting decisions. This would avoid contaminating decision-relevant costs with those that cannot change, regardless of the decision made. Financial "full costing" reports will, of course, continue to be produced for external financial reporting purposes. It is crucial to stress that "full product costing" for decision-making should include only those costs that are activity-specific and relevant to the given decision.

5.3 Product Portfolio and Pricing Decisions

The final question concerns costs that would be useful and relevant for deciding on alternative product mixes and determining product prices, assuming that *Duragen* should approach a capacity constraint and must reject some orders. The issues here are somewhat broader, however, because they permit management to determine which products are the major profit-drivers, and thus where opportunities for improved profit-making may lie.

A review of Table 11 indicates that the relevant costs are essentially limited to the out-of-pocket direct variable column, and possibly only to a subset of those. The indirect variable utilities charges and the indirect fixed recharges are allocations of common costs that are the same regardless of which product is produced. The depreciation charges are not relevant. The wastewater treatment costs vary with the product, but only to a limited extent. The market sale value of the by-products does vary because of the different efficiencies of the current manufacturing process. Obviously, all such calculations for long-range future planning should be made under the assumption that the company invests in new plant facilities, with the resulting change in costs.

Thus, although two-thirds or more of the costs identified in the current manufacturing cost schedule are relevant for the "invest or shut down" decision, only 39 percent or less are relevant to product portfolio decisions. Put differently, the costs that under the going concern assumption for *Duragen* will continue regardless of the products made (for example, direct fixed labor costs) are not relevant to the product mix decision. This latter point is important for *Duragen* because the yields vary substantially across the various products, and to the extent that the plant attempts a "full product costing" that absorbs all the fixed labor costs, the margins will be apparently higher or lower depending on the yields alone. Obviously, if the plant were operating at full capacity and contemplating producing only the lowest-yielding product, then yield would be an important factor. As the plant is not now capacity constrained, nor does it expect to be, this is not relevant here.

6. Conclusions

The general recommendation of this case study is to consider extending the computerized general ledger system to capture a richer set of the information currently available, preserving the economic nature of the data items (variable, fixed, out-of-pocket, historical, and so on) as the charges move through the system. Second, the company could expand the current traditional financial reporting focus of the system on "full absorption costing" to provide different types of cost schedules for different managerial decision contexts.

Dow Chemical has made some steps in this direction by establishing a business analysis group that currently provides such data on request to manufacturing units. The group has a keen awareness of the data quality and its relevance and usefulness for business decisions. Their analyses could be extended to develop more routine reporting systems for managers to use internally as they make various decisions of importance to the company.

Notes

1. Publicly available information is drawn from the Dow Chemical Company *Annual Report* 1993 and Form 10-K.
2. The Dow Chemical Company *Annual Report* 1992, p. 25.
3. Ibid., p. 14.

V.
ENVIRONMENTAL ACCOUNTING CASE STUDY: DU PONT

By David Shields, Miriam Heller, Devaun Kite,
and Beth Beloff

1. Background

E.I. du Pont de Nemours and Company was founded in Delaware in 1802. The company is organized in five major business segments: Petroleum (operating as Conoco), Chemicals, Fibers, Polymers, and Diversified Businesses. Du Pont is the largest chemical producer in the United States, and one of the world's largest, with consolidated 1993 sales of $37 billion.[1] Its operations outside the United States, spanning some 70 countries, account for about half its consolidated revenues.

The company employs approximately 110,000 people worldwide, a reduction of more than 20 percent over recent years. This downsizing has accompanied a major transition in management away from a traditional matrix structure in favor of a focus on two dozen strategic business units (SBUs). This is designed to integrate activities associated with the design, manufacture, and marketing of products that cut across sites, divisions, and geographical boundaries. At the same time, Du Pont is concentrating on reducing fixed costs and improving asset turnover to increase profitability and shareholder returns in a fiercely competitive global market.

In 1993, Du Pont spent approximately $500 million for capital projects related to environmental requirements and company goals.[2] Environmental expenses charged to current operations totaled about $1 billion in the same year. This includes the cost of operations, maintenance, depreciation, and research associated with

CASE HIGHLIGHTS: DU PONT

This case study of E.I. Du Pont de Nemours and Company, the largest chemical producer in the United States, focuses on an agricultural pesticide manufactured in LaPorte, Texas. The company's current efforts to develop an environmental cost accounting system at LaPorte are presented, followed by an estimate of the environmental costs of producing this pesticide. For a company that spends more than $1 billion a year on environmental protection, the importance of understanding environmental costs better cannot be overstated.

For the agricultural pesticide, over 19 percent of manufacturing costs are deemed "environmental." Almost one third of fixed manufacturing costs were determined to be environmental, compared with about 7 percent of the variable costs. But, the authors explain, some costs classified as fixed have a variable component. For this reason, the volume sensitivity of environmental costs may be understated.

The study describes how a better understanding of the nature of environmental costs can influence waste management decisions at the facility-level. When comparing the relative costs associated with waste management options, the company discovered that costs, as given by the accounting system, can be misleading. By focusing on incremental costs, Du Pont was able to realize real cost savings in the transition from deep-well injection to biological treatment of some process wastes.

This case study also shows how a company, armed with environmental cost accounting information, can make decisions that have a positive economic as well as environmental effect. For example, by comparing the projected reductions in waste against the estimated cost for several hundred corporate waste reduction initiatives, Du Pont was able to evaluate trade-offs between competing initiatives, while taking into account the company-wide leveraging of technological solutions.

—The editors

environmental activities, as well as accruals for future remediation. Approximately 80 percent of these costs arise in Du Pont's non-petroleum segments in the United States.

Du Pont's environmental record has drawn public criticism. Much of this can be traced to the company's top ranking in the Toxic Release Inventory (TRI), the national register of toxic chemical emissions and transfers. This, in turn, stems from Du Pont's long-standing reliance on deep-well injection (DWI) for the management of large volumes of process wastewater. More recently, some environmental observers have credited Du Pont with making significant progress toward its environmental goals.[3] For its part, Du Pont is committed to bringing about significant changes to improve environmental performance. In the words of Du Pont Chief Executive Officer E.S. Woolard Jr., in a 1993 report:

> It was four years ago that I first called for "corporate environmentalism," which I defined as "an attitude and performance commitment that place corporate stewardship fully in line with public desires and expectations." Some groups continue to direct criticism at our position on TRI and at our past practices. We ask them to focus on what we are doing now and on the direction we have clearly established for the future.[4]

This section discusses Du Pont's Corporate Environmental Plan, focusing on its approach for assigning priorities across multiple competing projects with environmental benefits. The case study focuses on one product—an important agricultural pesticide manufactured at the facility in LaPorte, Texas. Du Pont's current efforts to develop an environmental cost accounting system at LaPorte are presented, followed by an estimate of the environmental costs of producing this particular pesticide. Examples underscore the role of environmental cost information in waste management decisions and the value of more accurate information for product costing.

Du Pont's environmental commitment is embodied in the Corporate Environmental Plan (CEP), a company-wide approach to collecting environmental information, ensuring environmental compliance, meeting internal environmental goals, and assigning priorities to environmental initiatives. Du Pont has established and publicized a series of specific, quantifiable goals. For example, the company aims to reduce the release of carcinogenic air emissions in the year 2000 to 10 percent of 1987 levels across its U.S. facilities. Another goal is eliminating land disposal, including deep-well injection, of hazardous wastes by the end of this decade. To accomplish these and other environmental objectives cost-effectively, management has developed an approach to sorting and giving priority to the many potential options being identified throughout the company.

The CEP defines the operating tactics necessary to realize corporate environmental goals in a fashion compatible with business, technology, and manufacturing objectives. It provides guidelines to aid SBUs in devising specific environmental projects, primarily targeted at particular corporate policies, such as groundwater protection, or specific initiatives, such as spill containment diking. The issues and solutions that consitute the CEP are largely developed at the site level. This permits a certain amount of autonomy in decision-making, while ensuring organizational consistency.

The plan serves as the primary means for integrating environmental issues into business planning processes. After working through the annual process four times, Du Pont has experienced a cumulative learning effect. To date, more than 3,100 potential initiatives have been generated. For each of these the resources required, goals, applicable regulations, technologies, and program status are identified. An information network now enables communication and corporate roll-up across 115 sites. Of course, even if all of these proposed initiatives were worthwhile, the company must develop priorities for implementation. For example, some 700 of these offered waste-reduction benefits. To help select the most cost-effective projects, Du Pont developed a simple measure that compares the projected reduction in waste against the estimated cost of each initiative. These costs range from as little as 1¢ to as much as $1,000 per pound of waste reduced.[5]

To balance environmental commitments with business imperatives, Du Pont's method for rank-ordering environmental projects also allows for a consideration of regulatory and competitive factors. A general Pareto approach to cost-effectiveness has been adopted, which estimates that 80 percent of the total possible waste reduction can be accomplished for 20 percent of the total implementation cost. One benefit of this approach is that it offers a consistent and formal method for evaluating trade-offs among initiatives. For instance, the desirability of reducing the last pound of waste A can be weighed against the costs and benefits of reducing the first pound of waste B. Likewise, a system of priorities can extend to evaluating trade-offs over time—comparing trade-offs between current environmental initiatives and those that address future environmental regulations.

The timing of initiative implementation also takes into account business viability (from a competitive standpoint) and potential reductions in risk. Since the prioritization is in terms of pounds of waste generated, cross-media effects can be evaluated. All 3,000+ projects carry a "technology indicator" that allows for a meaningful grouping and leveraging of solutions. This helps identify potentially synergistic projects up-front in the evaluation process. To be considered in the prioritization process, each initiative is accompanied by an estimate of the implementation cost and the projected reduction in waste. This requires a method for tracking environmental costs and assigning them to business units.

This case study focuses on a pesticide manufactured by the Agriculture Products SBU at LaPorte, Texas. The LaPorte facility houses three other SBUs: Fluorochemicals, Specialty Chemicals, and Packaging and Industrial Polymers. Within each SBU, there are multiple related products. Many of these products are manufactured in stages, at multiple sites, creating the need for sophisticated management of the supply chain.

The relationship between SBUs and manufacturing plants reaches far beyond the single-product, single-site focus of this case study. Since products undergo partial manufacturing at several plants, the familiar logistical and transfer pricing problems of supply-chain management are introduced. In addition, the SBUs have tended to operate autonomously at LaPorte. Furthermore, within a given SBU there are often multiple products that sometimes share production facilities and can contribute to site-related management issues. This is particularly relevant in the case of environmental management. The shift toward greater reliance on SBUs can present difficulties in controlling and integrating the many activities occurring at a single plant site.

2. Environmental Cost Accounting at LaPorte

Du Pont's interest in environmental accounting stemmed from a desire to know the magnitude of the costs associated with meeting its corporate environmental objectives. This was particularly important for the comparative assessment of potential environmental projects. Furthermore, as Du Pont moves to a supply-chain management structure, managers have an even greater interest in information on the source of environmental costs throughout the product chain. Better information helps in assigning environmental costs to responsible business units and in driving the search for cheaper, more effective solutions.

The LaPorte site is pioneering the development of an environmental cost accounting system that is relatively unique in Du Pont. As a result, it is one of the best facilities for understanding actual environmental costs. Baseline determination of environmental costs at LaPorte involves a two-stage process. First, all costs labeled as environmental are isolated. Many of these "obvious" environmental costs relate to waste management involving incinerators, bio-treatment, steam strippers, deep-wells, environmental service contracts, and off-site waste handling. Regulatory compliance represents another relatively obvious cost. Second, environmental costs hidden within other costs are identified. For example, the time spent by non-environmental management on recurring environmental activities, which was formerly buried within the salary lines of SBU product cost sheets, is identified as an environmental cost.

Plant personnel at LaPorte believe this two-stage process successfully identifies about 90 percent of environmental costs. Some of the remaining unidentified costs are thought to be associated with maintenance and depreciation for environmental equipment, including flares, neutralization units, storage tanks, and closed-loop recycling processes. Based on the experiences of other companies, it is possible that this figure significantly understates the magnitude of total environmental costs. For example, many environmental activities performed by non-environmental employees may not be captured in this estimate.

After environmental costs are identified, they are separated into fixed and variable components to determine how they vary. A large portion of the total environmental costs appears to be fixed (both people and plant). Some Du Pont employees interviewed during this case study indicated that part of what is defined as fixed cost is actually variable. Examples cited include the cost of DWI maintenance, freight, contract waste disposal, and the dredging of wastewater treatment basins.

Other costs that are labeled "fixed" with respect to production volume can vary with other activities. Thus, some investments may actually reduce environmental costs for Du Pont, but this will not be reflected in the cost charged to products due to limitations in the cost tracking system. Although these constraints exist, corporate requirements for fixed-cost reductions create motivation for more accurate identification.

Finally, costs are divided into controllable and non-controllable categories. Most fixed costs are non-controllable in the short term, which means they can only be managed through capital investment or long-term utilization decisions. The ability of management to reduce short-term costs seems to be limited.

While some environmental costs arise within SBUs, each unit also shares costs from the Environmental Control area. These common environmental costs are allocated to SBUs in proportion to the projected waste-flow rates. Central facility costs are also allocated based on investments, number of people, time spent, and so on. The inexact nature of these estimates and the importance of these allocations to product control and costing have led to efforts to determine each product's use of common facilities more accurately. For example, meters have been installed to determine the progress toward waste minimization goals, allowing some allocations to be based on actual flow rather than estimates. This represents a great improvement in that waste reduction has generated measurable cost savings.

Du Pont expects managers to achieve the best possible rate of return on capital investments. Environmental projects often have a special urgency, derived from both government regulation and corporate environmental imperatives. If a capital investment is necessitated by a legal requirement, it will be undertaken without regard to the internal rate of return. For discretionary investments, however, incomplete identification of environmental costs and benefits makes it difficult to accurately capture the economics associated with an environmentally related investment. This problem should ease as the environmental cost accounting system becomes fully operational.

Although many different accounting systems exist across Du Pont sites, the company is moving toward an integrated system for all sites. Despite budgeting and other setbacks, implementation of such a system is scheduled for 1995. Among its many capabilities, this will allow for better identification of environmental costs and assignment to SBUs, processes, and products. This enables a more accurate assignment of environmental costs through detailed decomposition of production inputs using more appropriate allocation bases.

Du Pont's efforts to determine environmental costs at LaPorte have provided insights into their origins. Table 13 summarizes the largest contributors to the environmental costs at the site. These costs cover the wide variety of activities implicit in environmental management at LaPorte, including materials, labor, management, and capital expenditures. The largest category, "other," includes taxes, fees, laboratory work, training, and legal costs. This is followed by depreciation expenses, operations, and off-site, contract waste disposal.

Table 13. Estimated Site Environmental Costs (in percent)

Other (incl. taxes, fees, training, legal)	21.0
Depreciation	16.8
Operations	13.9
Contract Waste Disposal	12.4
Utilities	11.9
Salaries	9.6
Maintenance	8.5
Engineering Services	6.0
Total	**100.0**

3. Product Environmental Cost Analysis

Manufacture of this agricultural pesticide at the LaPorte facility generates liquid wastes, solid residues, and air emissions. Some process wastewater has traditionally been managed through DWI, a practice that has come under increasing regulatory and public scrutiny in recent years. Some of this wastewater can be treated at the shared, on-site biological treatment facility. Other streams are incinerated in the shared central scrubbed incinerator (CSI). In addition, a number of toxic substances are involved as reactants or intermediates.

Other off-site environmental implications, such as those arising from product use or the management of used packaging, were excluded from this analysis. Final manufacturing occurs at LaPorte, where the product is packaged in bulk. Formulation and repackaging in paper containers occurs in various locations around the world. As the product tends to clump, the contaminated packaging must be broken, making reuse impossible. Du Pont recommends that the used packaging be incinerated, and is currently evaluating the use of reusable containers.

Based on a projected annual production volume for 1993, Figure 14 presents the product's environmental cost as a percentage of total manufacturing cost. The relative portions of fixed and variable costs are also shown for environmental and non-environmental manufacturing costs. At current production levels, environmental costs account for 19.1 percent of total manufacturing cost; a significant portion of this appears to be fixed. In fact, environmental costs represent approximately 31 percent of the total fixed costs for this product. In contrast, variable environmental costs represent only 7.4 percent of the product's total variable manufacturing cost.

Since, by definition, fixed costs remain constant with changes in production, environmental costs are unlikely to be a significant factor in any decision to increase or lower production. Despite this label, however, these costs can vary. In addition, some fixed costs may continue if production is stopped. For example, the product shares production facilities with other agricultural products, which would presumably continue to use the facilities that contribute de-

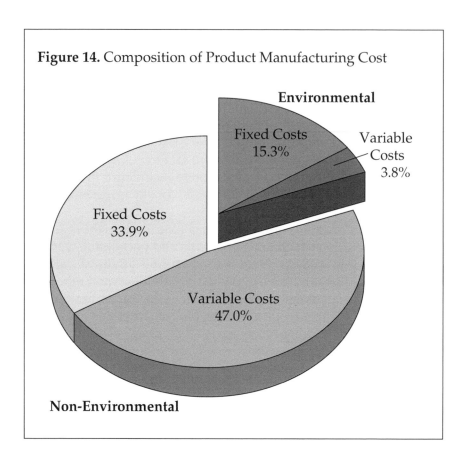

Figure 14. Composition of Product Manufacturing Cost

preciation charges to the product. These calculations are based on the environmental costs that have already been identified by Du Pont.

4. Uses of Environmental Cost Information

The preponderance of fixed costs in total environmental costs may cause confusion regarding the relative costs of alternative waste management technologies. This is because under full-absorption costing (in which all production costs are allocated to units of production), some alternatives that appear costlier than others may actually generate fewer incremental costs (e.g., by making use of existing facilities). This is often the case when new methods of treating waste render equipment or facilities useless. Unless the existing equipment or facilities can profitably be disposed of, there is no true fixed cost savings. Stated another way, the out-of-pocket cost of pollution prevention alternatives may not correspond to the accounting cost per unit of these alternatives. The correct decision criterion is to minimize the out-of-pocket costs and to ignore "sunk costs," such as depreciation, that are incurred under all alternatives.

One example of the misleading nature of sunk costs (and the effect of sunk costs on internally reported accounting costs) was provided by the Agriculture Products manager. The LaPorte site has several alternatives for waste treatment and disposal. The criteria for determining which to use include cost per pound, effect on TRI, risk of future liability, and degree to which the method of disposal is acceptable to stakeholders. Figure 15 indicates the variable cost per pound for treating wastewater using a variety of methods. Du Pont based this analysis on the assumption that DWI could actually be shut down. As a result, some fixed costs such as freight, maintenance, engineering, and personnel, will either diminish or disappear. For comparison, the full-absorption cost has been superimposed for the bio-treatment and DWI options. A focus on the full-absorption cost suggests DWI is the least cost option, at 0.09¢ per pound. In contrast, by focusing on variable costs, it became apparent that bio-treatment, at only 0.03¢ per pound, resulted in a lower out-of-pocket cost. This represents a saving of 0.04¢ per pound over DWI.

The results presented in Figure 15 were particularly revealing to Du Pont because DWI had previously been assumed the least expensive approach. This misconception stemmed from the way the depreciation of the facility had been factored into the unit cost of bio-treatment. The current accounting system charges each SBU with the full-absorption cost of bio-treatment, based on actual use. In other words, the cost per pound of bio-treatment is the total cost (variable and fixed) of the bio-treatment facility, divided by the total number of pounds processed. This provided an incentive to divert waste to DWI, where the full-absorption cost is lower. Unfortunately, in reducing the demand for bio-treatment, the cost per

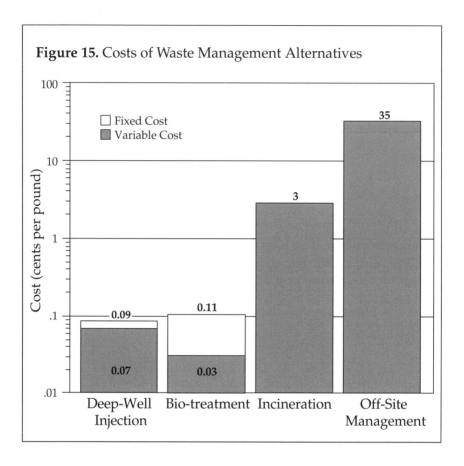

Figure 15. Costs of Waste Management Alternatives

pound increases for those still relying on it. This leads to an even lower demand for bio-treatment, and so on.

In this case, allocating the full cost of bio-treatment leads to a suboptimal result for Du Pont because it discourages its use. The cost savings is an illusion, because the fixed costs of bio-treatment are incurred anyway; the cost of the plant has already been incurred. This illusion is further reinforced if the analysis is conducted on a cost per pound of total organic carbon (as opposed to the cost per pound of wastewater). The corresponding values for bio-treatment and DWI then become $2.80 and 60¢ per pound of total organic content, respectively.

The above cost information was determined in a feasibility study for phasing out DWI in accord with corporate objectives. Research and Development personnel charged with identifying ways to discontinue DWI completely found no technical impediments to using bio-treatment for all the waste generated. This was partly made possible by Du Pont's recent success in lowering the organic loading in wastewater streams. The next step is a plant pilot test, which is in its early stages. If the pilot study is successful, DWI will be discontinued.

The impact of this revised approach will be a reduction of variable costs and a continuation of the same level of fixed costs. This is an example of how environmental cost accounting information may help in rethinking the management of hazardous wastes. The analysis also facilitates discontinuing DWI, thus lowering Du Pont's releases to land, in accord with corporate environmental goals.

Despite the organization of manufacturing capability at LaPorte into distinct SBUs, problems remain with the allocation of environmental costs to specific products. These occur because within each SBU there are shared units and resources for different products, and, in many cases, inadequate or non-existent metering of inputs and outputs. A good example of this is found in the Agricultural Products SBU, with respect to the central scrubbed incinerator. Previously, there was no attempt to estimate the relative contribution of wastes from the various agricultural products treated by the CSI. However, some staff suspected that the agricultural pesticide contributed disproportionately to the waste stream. If this were true, it would have the effect of under-allocating costs to the product and over-allocating costs to other agricultural products. These costing distortions could, in turn, affect both transfer prices and within-plant conversion costs, thus leading to incorrect marketing and production decisions.

Recently, the facility developed metering capabilities to capture more accurately the quantities of waste contributed by the various products. The resulting waste measures have had an immediate effect on management, because the results were so surprising. Once clear, accurate information about the volume of waste was available, steps were immediately taken to reduce the waste, primarily through "good housekeeping" methods and by improving capital productivity. Furthermore, accurate measurement of waste generation may lead to more precise determination of the environmental costs to be associated with each product.

This more precise information is particularly important given the responsibility of supply-chain managers for the profitability of their products, as it provides an impartial and accurate measurement of the resources required to process wastes. Supply-chain managers compete with each other about profit performance, so any attempt to improve the accuracy of measurement should result in more equitable allocations. The metering project has also resulted in reduced waste generation and lower operating costs for the CSI. The cost allocation improvements driven by the metering application may also lead to production decisions that will further reduce the out-of-pocket cost of operating the CSI.

In addition, a cooperative effort between the Agricultural Products group and the Specialty Chemicals group has resulted in a mutually beneficial arrangement that will reduce the incineration costs of both groups. Formerly, a major (variable) cost of operating the CSI was the purchase of natural gas to fuel the incinerator. At the same time, the Specialty Chemicals unit incinerated a waste stream with very high energy content. Redirecting the waste from Specialty Chemicals to the CSI would lower natural gas requirement and permit the Specialty Chemicals incinerator to shut down. As of this date, Du Pont has completed an internal demonstration of the feasibility of this approach, with promising environmental and operational results.

5. Conclusions

The LaPorte facility has demonstrated the feasibility of identifying, isolating, and using environmental cost information in a practical business context. For a company that spends more than $1 billion a year on environmental protection, the importance of understanding environmental costs better cannot be overstated.

Furthermore, this case study illustrates how better understanding of the environmental costs associated with the manufacture of a single product and other on-site activities can facilitate the integration of environmental and other business objectives. This can yield benefits at the facility level, from the standpoint of SBU management, and in the corporation at large.

LaPorte management has made considerable progress in identifying the sources of these environmental costs. However, some potentially significant sources of these costs are not included in the current estimates. There are practical limits to how far these other components might be quantified. Probably more than 10 percent of environmental costs remain unidentified, especially considering the value of raw materials that become waste.

Efforts to date have concentrated on the environmental costs that arise from operations and maintenance activities. Although these costs are among the easiest to identify and quantify, they are a subset of the total. For example, they exclude the effect of current activity on future liability, hidden regulatory costs, and the less tangible costs and benefits of current environmental activity in terms of attitudes of customers, shareholders, the community, and other stakeholders.

The results of the environmental cost study indicate that environmental costs at LaPorte tend to be fixed rather than variable. In fact, almost one-third of the total fixed manufacturing costs of one product were determined to be environmental, compared with about 7 percent of the variable costs. This indicates that the environmental costs are probably not volume-sensitive. However, as discussed earlier, it is commonly believed that some costs classified as fixed have a non-trivial variable component. Thus, the volume sensitivity of environmental costs may be understated. In addition, fixed costs tend to respond to changes in capital equipment, process flow, and similar major changes rather than to variations in volume.

This case study has demonstrated how, armed with environmental cost accounting information, a company can make decisions that have a positive economic as well as environmental effect. Environmental cost information was used to develop cost-benefit measures for evaluating various options for improving environmental performance. By comparing the projected reductions in waste against the estimated cost of each initiative, it was possible to evaluate trade-offs between competing initiatives while taking into account such factors as cross-media effects.

This study also describes how a better understanding of the nature of environmental costs can influence waste management decisions. When comparing the relative costs associated with various waste management options, the company discovered that costs, as given by the accounting system, can be misleading. Management must continue to consider the incremental cost of alternatives rather than the full costs reported by the traditional accounting system.

Notes

1. E.I. Du Pont de Nemours and Company, *1993 Annual Report* (Wilmington, Del.: 1994).
2. Ibid.
3. Eric Steedman, Sean Moulton, and Sara Baerwald, "America's Least Wanted: The 1994 Campaign for Cleaner Corporations," *Council for Economic Priorities Research Report,* November/December 1994.
4. E.I. Du Pont de Nemours and Company, *Corporate Environmentalism: Progress Report* (Wilmington, Del.: 1993).
5. H. Dale Martin, "Environmental Planning: Balancing Environmental Commitments with Economic Realities," in Global Environmental Management Institute, *Environmental Management in a Global Economy* (Washington, D.C.: 1994), pp. 57–64.

VI.
ENVIRONMENTAL ACCOUNTING CASE STUDY: S.C. JOHNSON WAX

By Ajay Maindiratta and Rebecca Todd

1. Introduction

S.C. Johnson Wax (SCJ), a privately held corporation, was founded in 1886 as a maker of parquet flooring. The company expanded within a few years to floor-care preparations, and is now among the world's leading providers of chemical specialty products for the home and workplace. The North American Consumer Products division (NACP), whose product portfolio is found in Table 14, markets some of its most familiar brands. SCJ also has a major presence in the commercial market for similar products.

The company operates in 49 countries with nearly 13,000 employees, including more than 3,500 in the United States. As it is privately held, financial information regarding sales and earnings is not published. Thus, relative size, growth rates, and other financial statistics are unavailable.

Some SCJ products have attracted public and regulatory interest on environmental grounds due to the active ingredients, delivery solvents, or packaging technologies used. The company has a publicly stated commitment to prevent and reduce wastes. In 1975, it was the first manufacturer to voluntarily discontinue worldwide use of CFC propellants in its aerosols.

This case study examines the Insect Control Business of NACP in order to critically evaluate SCJ's environmental management accounting, given the types of environmental issues and consequent business imperatives the company faces. It also reports on an

CASE HIGHLIGHTS: S.C. JOHNSON WAX

This case study looks at the Insect Control Business of S.C. Johnson Wax, one of the leading providers of chemical specialty products for the home and workplace. Most of the environmental challenges arise in product registration, marketing, and post-consumer product management (such as recycling of aerosol cans). Proliferating state regulations on pesticide labeling and use represent a major issue for the company. Regulation affects lead times for registering products and developing formulations, which in turn affects the incentive to develop new active ingredients.

Some executives expressed concern that effective cost management may suffer because the demand placed on resources by environmental issues is not adequately reflected in the organization's management accounting systems. Longer term strategic planning and control, rather than shorter term operating and tactical decisions, are most likely to be affected by environmental information gaps.

The environmental cost analysis done for one household pesticide product found that environment-related expenses for marketing and R&D could be a significant fraction of the total operating expenses. Waste processing and the other costs of the factory's environmental departments are negligible—a mere 0.25 percent of the manufacturing cost-of-sales. But about 17 percent of marketing administration and about 21 percent of personnel expenses for this product can be attributed to the environment. The authors recommend that S.C. Johnson construct statements that segment the firm along lines that reflect key environmental concerns, as a supplement to the profitability statements now used.

—The editors

Table 14. S.C. Johnson Wax North American Consumer Products

Home Care	Insect Control
Floor Care & Cleaners	Base Raid
Future	Ant & Roach
Step Saver	Fogger
Brite	House & Garden
Armstrong	Fumigator
Bathroom Care	Flying Insect Killer
Toilet Duck	Wasp & Hornet
Bathroom Duck	Yard Guard
Furniture Care	Flea Killer Plus
Pledge	Flea Killer
Favor	Ant Baits
Household Cleaner	Roach Baits
Air Care	Home Insect Killer
Glade Aerosol	Ant & Roach Liquid
Glade Carpet & Room	Trigger
Glade Plug–Ins	Ant & Roach Home Insect
Glade Pottery	Killer
Glade Clip–Ons	Max Raid
Drackett	OFF!
Windex	OFF! Aerosol
Vanish	Deep Woods OFF!
Drano	Deep Woods OFF!
Carpet Science	Sportsmen
Mr. Muscle	OFF! Skintastic
Twinkle	

Personal Care

Skin Care	Derm
Edge Gel	Aveeno
Edge Aftershave	Rhuli
Skintimate	

environmental cost analysis of one household pesticide product available in various sizes. Environmental cost here includes resources used anywhere in the organization as a consequence of the environmental dimensions of the business. Environmental management accounting systems are those that help by directing attention, providing decision support, and facilitating management control via appropriate financial and non-financial analyses and presentations.

2. Market Context, Responsibility, and Accountability for Key Business Decisions

The Consumer Products business, which accounts for a large proportion of SCJ's operations, is highly competitive and very sensitive to consumer perceptions. As a marketing-focused company, SCJ's lines of business are defined with respect to product markets. Thus, the innovation and creativity driving sales have historically been largely vested in identifying and marketing quality products that have a distinct "plus" for the consumer. The company relies on in-house scientists and engineers, as well as basic technologies developed in other industries including chemicals, pharmaceuticals, and agricultural products, to bring forward new and better products.

A simplified organizational chart is presented in Figure 16. The Corporate office of Worldwide Consumer Products (WWCP) is involved in longer-term strategic choices and planning. The Businesses (i.e., the marketing arms) have been given primary authority for key short- and medium-term decisions, including pricing, product offerings, and product formulations. For instance, the pesticides sold by Insect Control are formulated in either aqueous or organic solvent bases. Since water-based formulations may be slightly slower to act than solvent-based ones, U.S. consumers misperceive them to be less efficacious, which could prompt unnecessary overuse. As a result, many of SCJ's U.S. Insect Control products are solvent-based despite the more complex regulatory issues raised by such a formulation.

Similarly, Insect Control ultimately decides—based on consumer input—whether aerosols, sprays, or continuous action technologies will be offered, and which product mixes and volumes

Figure 16. S.C. Johnson Wax Organizational Chart

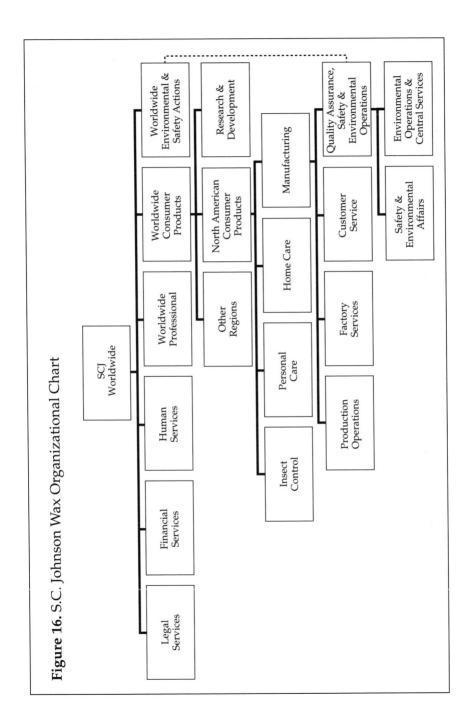

will be produced. All other segments of the organization, including Manufacturing, Legal, and R&D, are seen as servicing the Businesses. The impact of the Businesses and the accountability for their decisions are reflected in the preparation of (more or less) full-cost product profitability reports for defined groups of products in each line of business.

3. Environmental Aspects of the Insect Control Business

3.1 Profile

This section briefly profiles the environmental aspects of the Insect Control business, with a particular focus on the production at Waxdale, SCJ's primary manufacturing facility in Wisconsin. The potential exposure from environmentally related issues is significant for Insect Control products. For instance, the active pesticide ingredients, which account for less than 1 percent on average of the total product formula, are selected for their efficacy on specific insects. Many are derived from natural sources and approved for household use, yet are often mistakenly categorized as on a par with agricultural pesticides. As the manufacturer, SCJ must comply with pesticide registration requirements, state and federal labeling regulations, and guidelines for safe handling, storage, and disposal.

In addition, both the production and use of organic solvents result in volatile organic compound (VOC) emissions. Further, the Fire Protection Association, on behalf of the national insurance industry, categorizes the flammability potential of these products depending on the amount and kind of solvent they contain. Hence, there are restrictions on their transportation and storage.

Some local household hazardous waste (HHW) collection programs mistakenly collect used pesticide containers even though household products are specifically exempted from federal regulations for hazardous waste disposal under Subtitle C of the Resource Conservation and Recovery Act (RCRA). The potential for a patchwork of state and local disposal restrictions exists if more HHW programs list and collect pesticide containers. In addition, following a "cradle-to-grave" philosophy, manufacturers are increasingly likely to be held accountable for creating products that are environmentally responsible in use and disposal.

The production and filling of Insect Control products is done at SCJ's Waxdale facility. The handling of raw materials and the cleaning of filling lines for product change-overs can generate wastewater with hazardous and non-hazardous contaminants as well as solid wastes, such as defective cans or plastic packages that are crushed and recycled after the recovery of their contents. Filling the products contributes significantly to the total VOC air emissions from the facility. This is important since the facility is located in the severe ozone non-attainment region that encompasses Chicago and Milwaukee.

The image of some SCJ products may improve as more state recycling mandates are imposed. In particular, as policy-makers and the public become better informed on aerosol can recyclability, states may be less likely to adopt inappropriate disposal regulations or taxes specific to aerosols.

3.2 Environmental Issues and Trade-offs

This section takes a closer look at the major environment-related issues confronting Insect Control in order to derive SCJ's business imperatives and informational needs. For the purposes of demonstration, one issue is analyzed in greater depth by identifying possible responses and associated advantages and disadvantages. Many environmental issues are pressing only because of their interactions with other environmental and non-environmental issues; some of these are identified below.

One pressing issue is the proliferation of state regulations concerning pesticide distribution and usage. Related issues include the lead times for product registration, the lead times for developing formulations, and the reduced incentive to develop new active ingredients because of dis-economies of scale. Four possible responses can be identified:

1) *Develop State-specific Formulations*
   Disadvantages:
   - economically infeasible
   - uncertainty about future regulatory developments complicates interim planning

145

- once enacted, regulations tend to increase the compliance burden
- logistical problems increase
- inventory and distribution management problems increase (increased inventories, increased obsolescence, shipments diverted to wrong state, and associated safe disposal problems)
- waste management demands increase due to more frequent cleaning out of production lines
- R&D resources have to be devoted to developing multiple formulations and to registering them
- retail and industry distribution system is not structured to state lines

Advantages:
- product efficacy can be maintained
- maximizes opportunity for state-by-state market penetration

2) *Develop Common Denominator Formulations*
Disadvantages:
- uncertainty about future regulatory developments complicates interim planning
- developing lowest common denominator formulation may sacrifice product efficacy (and revenue and market share slippage and reduced public health benefit could occur)

Advantages:
- lacks the disadvantages of the state-specific response

3) *Promote Common Regulations Across States*
Disadvantages:
- calls for costly legislative intervention
- standardized regulations would eliminate registration complexity, which is a current barrier to additional industry competition

Advantages:
- provides a degree of control over regulatory uncertainties, thereby improving the odds of being able to supply the market with common, yet effective formulation

4) *Promote Federal Preemption of State Laws*

Another issue that needs to be addressed in an environmental context is the problems posed by solvent-based formulations in production and customer use. Related issues in this case include customer perceptions about performance of aqueous-based formulations and VOC emissions. The possible responses are eliminating solvent-based formulations, doing more to address and control the environmental impacts of solvent-based formulations, and improving consumer perception of aqueous-based formulations.

Similarly, the production of VOC emissions in a severe ozone non-attainment region can be considered. Possible responses include buying VOC credits, expanding the use of soil-bioreactor treatment technology to break down the organic compounds, improving or controlling filling technologies to reduce emissions, and changing product formulations to reduce or eliminate solvents that contribute to VOC emissions.

A fourth issue is organizational responsibility for end-of-life (and damaged) hazardous product reclamation and disposal. One possible response is to contract for these services locally; the disadvantages of this course include expense and the potential for unanticipated costs related to unsafe disposal by local companies. Another response could be to contract for transporters to return the product to SCJ. The disadvantages include the potential for unanticipated costs related to transport. A third response could be to educate and work with municipalities and consumers on safe disposal methods.

Another issue of concern is the uncertainty about how long current ingredients can be used before future regulatory action restricts their use. Related issues in this case include the drying up of the pipeline of new active ingredients and the lead times for registration and formulation.

3.3 Environment-Driven Activities at SCJ

The paramount importance of environmental concerns to SCJ is manifest in the top-level office of the VP Worldwide for Environmental and Safety Actions. The broad functions of this office are:

(i)   setting Environmental & Safety (E&S) policies worldwide (for both products and production process);

(ii) setting specific long-term goals and objectives for E&S programs worldwide, and development and monitoring of the related businesses' strategic action plans;

(iii) governmental relations; and,

(iv) communication with employees and the public on environmental and safety matters.

A key product-specific activity this office performs is maintenance of the material safety data sheets, a database that is valuable in responding to consumer inquiries about environmental and safety issues associated with specific products.

Activities carried out to reduce environmental exposure via product reformulation/new product introduction and activities carried out for product registration and ongoing compliance are of particular significance to Insect Control. The major actors here are R&D, the Businesses, and the Corporate WWCP office. (SCJ relies on its bulk chemical suppliers to develop active ingredients, conduct necessary toxicology testing of the actives, and get them on the approved list.)

In-house Legal and Government Compliance departments provide a wide range of support for environmental and compliance-related issues, such as product registration, permits (e.g., for air emissions, water effluents, and hazardous waste disposal), and possible Superfund involvement. Many other environmental activities and reporting requirements in the United States are carried out by the Environmental Operations department and the Safety and Environmental Affairs department within North American Manufacturing at Waxdale. The wastewater treatment, solid waste, and trash handling facilities are common for all of Waxdale. The facility also operates a waste-to-energy facility with two of its plant boilers for recovering high BTU factory waste, and a soil-bioreactor system for breaking down isobutane and propane to reduce VOC emissions.

4. Environment-Related Business Imperatives and Perceived Information Gaps

It is evident from the discussion in the previous sections that Insect Control's environmental dimensions are integral to the business. It

is also evident that these connote a complex, changing, and uncertain arena, framed by:
- regulations and constraints,
- escalating and uncertain fees,
- long lead times for registration and approval,
- evolving consumer perceptions and values,
- emerging "cradle-to-grave" stewardship obligations,
- unpredictability of the useful life of actives and other ingredients, and
- liability and litigation.

These are coupled with other business realities, such as:
- consumer perceptions about product efficacy,
- long lead times in developing formulations, and
- a dwindling stream of approved active ingredients.

These issues pose a special challenge to the managerial functions of planning, performance evaluation, and management control. There is a strong sense in the organization that environmental issues require a significant amount of resources, especially personnel time. Key executives are concerned that effective cost management here may be hampered by the fact that this demand on resources is not being adequately and comprehensively reflected and communicated in the organization's management accounting systems. There is also a concern that the resulting information gaps hinder managers and employees from responding to environmental imperatives effectively, efficiently, and appropriately throughout the organization. Through discussions, it also became clear that knowledge about and sensitivity to environmental issues and the trade-offs they implied were not perceived to be uniform throughout the organization among decision makers. Several managers felt that more internal communication was essential.

Several managerial functions are most affected by these information gaps. It is evident from the earlier discussion that longer-term strategic planning and control (anticipating the future and positioning the organization for it, and motivating people to do the same), are key functions that are affected. It would also appear, given the market and operating context described in earlier sections, that shorter-term operating and tactical decisions are practically not affected by these information gaps. Discussions with key executives in Manufacturing, R&D, Corporate Strategic Planning, Environmental and Safety Actions, the Controller's Office, and the Insect Control Business seemed to support this conclusion. For instance, Insect Control's management does not see improvements in full product cost accuracy, from the level currently available, as being terribly important for short- to medium-term pricing or product portfolio decisions. These decisions follow much more from tactical considerations. Similarly, Operating Management does not see such improvements as being relevant for short- to medium-term production decisions.

5. SCJ's Existing Management Accounting System

SCJ's management accounting system culminates in the preparation of historical, full-cost profitability statements at the level of a product group. Full-cost statements imply that all costs are charged to business segments either via cost-of-goods-sold or operating expenses. In general, charges may arrive either through direct attribution (which covers a significant portion of total expenses) or cost allocations. As with any system that is based on the allocation of expenses, the dollar number in the resulting bottom line can be questioned because of the allocation bases chosen for particular items. Otherwise, every expense of doing business appears somewhere in the line items.

Historical cost statements imply that the usual accrual accounting procedures for external reporting are followed. Thus, actual or standard charges include accounting depreciation on the original acquisition cost of long-term resources rather than opportunity costs. No product-specific charges appear for the use (as opposed to acquisition) of facility-wide quasi-resources, such as the permit capacity to discharge particular effluents.

Very briefly, SCJ's management accounting system has the following features. The product is transferred from manufacturing at Waxdale to the Businesses at standard full manufacturing product cost. The transferred cost includes all raw materials, package components, and production expenses incurred at Waxdale (including accounting depreciation and all costs of its environment-related departments and facilities).

The two major corporate service departments, Legal and R&D, also charge Businesses a standard full hourly rate for identifiable services rendered and projects undertaken. In the case of the Legal department, this is done only for tasks that involve more than 100 hours. The rest of legal and non-project R&D is added to the set of corporate expense pools, which are comprehensive and include the expenses of Worldwide Environmental and Safety Actions.

Costs in the various corporate expense pools are allocated using a variety of allocation bases, through intermediate organizational levels, to the Businesses. The Businesses pass on to their product groups, those legal and R&D charges that are readily identifiable with the product groups, with some exceptions. All other administrative costs (including marketing, legal, R&D, business expenses, and remaining higher-level allocations and charges) are allocated to product groups on the basis of sales dollars.

6. Environmental Cost of a Household Pesticide Product

Table 15 provides an environmental cost analysis for one household pesticide product. The specific product considered is only one of several aerosols produced in Waxdale, and the aerosol production lines are only one part of the manufacturing facility. The first column presents key figures from the product profitability statement (expressed as a percent of net sales). The next column isolates the environmental costs that were aggregated by the existing accounting system into the various profit and loss line items. The last column presents the impact of the environmental costs not captured in the existing accounting system.

The estimation procedures for this analysis were based on interviews with department personnel, their self-audits of time spent in environmental activities, and source documents such as departmental expense statements and manufacturing overhead studies. There are several areas in Sales, R&D, and Administrative Management that were probably driven to a material extent by environmental concerns, but the contribution of these could not be estimated.

The environmental cost analysis revealed that waste processing and the other costs of the manufacturing facility's environmen-

Table 15. Environmental Cost (as a Percent of Net Sales)

Description	Profit & Loss Statement	Environmental Pool Costs	Additional Environmental Costs
Sales	100%	–	–
Cost of Sales	45%	0.11%[1]	0.02%[3]
Gross Profit	55%	–	–
Operating Expenses	53%	1.42%[2]	0.85%[4]
Total Operating Profit	2%		

1. Estimated waste processing costs and other expenses of the manufacturing facility.
2. Estimated manufacturing personnel and overhead related to environmental initiatives.
3. Includes estimated registration fees and mill taxes, environmental R&D projects, allocated Environmental and Safety Actions expenses, and directly identifiable legal expenses.
4. Estimated marketing personnel time spent on environmental concerns.

tal departments are negligible—a mere 0.25 percent of the manufacturing cost-of-sales. In contrast, the environment-related functional expenses for marketing and R&D could be a significant fraction of the total operating expenses. Marketing management was able to assess the time spent on environmental concerns by its staff, and thus a clear picture of the total environmental component of this item is possible. Altogether about 17 percent of marketing administration can be directly attributed to the environment (registration fees and mill taxes) per existing accounting systems and about 21 percent can be attributed to the environment for personnel expenses (including wages and salaries), which are not recognized as environmental in the current accounting system.

7. Evaluation and Recommendations

The various statements prepared as steps in the management accounting and reporting exercise described in Section 5—for instance, the manufacturing overhead accumulation and allocation schedules, and the product profitability statements—are the only management accounting reports identified by this case study at SCJ. This was then evaluated in terms of the attention-directing, decision-supporting, and decision-influencing (i.e., motivation and control) roles of management accounting systems, from the standpoint of the environment-related business imperatives identified earlier. This evaluation leads to a set of recommendations for modifying and supplementing the existing system to better serve managerial information needs.

To begin, it is important to note that the existing system is a full-cost one, and thus every historical cost of doing business appears somewhere in the line items of the product profitability statements, albeit perhaps aggregated into a broad expense category such as cost-of-goods-sold or marketing administration. Although information losses due to the practices followed for cost accumulation and aggregation, along with distortions in product profitability numbers due to the practices followed for tracing and allocating costs, certainly need to be evaluated, there is otherwise "nothing missing" from a product's bottom line.

In evaluating the information losses and the product profitability distortions, it is important to consider if they significantly affect the attention-directing contributions of the system, have decision consequences, and significantly weaken the effectiveness of the motivation and control contributions of the system. These assessments and the associated recommendations are made while keeping cost-benefit considerations in mind.

As regards attention-directing contributions, it was noted earlier that management of environmental issues at SCJ is hampered by the fact that the resulting demand on organizational resources is not adequately highlighted by the current accounting systems.

Two reasons can be identified for this shortcoming. First, the identity of even the obvious environmental costs—for instance, waste processing—gets lost as numbers are aggregated and move through the current system. Second, and more important in dollar terms (as shown by the environmental cost analysis in Section 6), many costs accumulated in non-environmental cost pools are significantly driven by environmental concerns but never flagged as such. Most notable here are personnel-related costs. For instance, marketing personnel devote considerable time and energy (estimated by managers to be a little above 20 percent) to environmental issues related to their current and planned product offerings. Compensation for these activities is, however, simply classified as marketing salaries and wages. These observations lead to the first two recommendations.

Recommendation 1: Make simple modifications to the cost aggregation process and the subsequent transmission of numbers through the accounting system. These changes should be aimed at preserving the identity of dollars that are unambiguously environmental as they flow through the system. For instance, the standard cost of production could pass through from manufacturing to the Businesses as two numbers, thus keeping separate the dollar amount for the part of the manufacturing burden related to environmental activities such as waste treatment. The result would be to show cost-of-goods-sold on the product profitability statements as the sum of two numbers. Similarly, the expenses of the VP Worldwide for Environmental and Safety Actions would maintain their identity instead of being incorporated into other cost pools as they are allocated downward to the profitability statements. Although a goal of each R&D project is to realize environmental improvement, those with a major focus on the environment would continue to be labeled as such.

This first recommendation makes some contribution to improving existing product profitability statements as vehicles for communicating the impact of environment-related activities on the Businesses. However, it does not address the more sizable expenses that are significantly driven by environmental issues but not accumulated in environmentally labeled accounts. Identification of the environmental contribution to these expenses would require some degree of activity analysis. The following recommendation addresses this.

Recommendation 2: Through self-audits, have relevant personnel periodically assess the extent to which non-environmental costs in their jurisdiction are driven by environmental activities, and present this information for each such line item in a supplementary column to the product profitability statement. Although imperfect and subject to self-reporting biases, this would nevertheless be a useful instrument for directing attention to and monitoring trends in environment-driven resource consumption.

Turning to decision support, it was noted in Section 4 that short- to medium-term decisions about production resource allocation, pricing, and product portfolios are all driven by tactical marketing considerations and do not rely on environmental product cost numbers. Thus neither product cost distortions due to the fact that some chosen cost-tracing and allocation practices do not faithfully mirror cause and effect, nor the fact that product costs impound historical rather than opportunity costs for the use of capacity resources, are critical for operating and tactical decisions.

The discussion in Section 4 also identified longer-term strategic planning as an important environmental-related business imperative. A key question in the strategic planning exercise is: What businesses is the company running? Answering this question requires recognition that firms are multidimensional entities. A product-market focus may lead to one answer, a technology focus might lead to a second, an inputs-processing focus might lead to something else, and so on. Whatever the answer, historical cost statements can serve as useful attention-directing instruments and starting points in the strategic planning exercise, provided they are appropriately constructed.

From a product-market focus, it may indeed be most useful to view SCJ in terms of the current business designations. In terms of environmental concerns and imperatives, however, another segmentation may be more enlightening for understanding the overall business. For instance, solvent-based products are sold by several businesses and are a major environmental concern. What are the implications to SCJ of being in the business of selling solvent-based products? This cannot be easily extracted from the current set of product profitability statements, but a great deal could be learned from a set of statements that separate SCJ into aqueous and solvent-based products. Similarly, since many environmental concerns are related to particular active ingredients that are used in products sold by several businesses, SCJ could be segmented into lines of actives. This leads to the next recommendation.

Recommendation 3: As a supplement to existing product-market-focused profitability statements, construct statements that segment the firm along lines that are more natural from the perspective of key environmental concerns. To avoid the distortions due to arbitrary cost allocations, the statements should be prepared on the segment-margin basis rather than the full-cost basis.

Another recommendation to support longer-term strategic planning, particularly since there is some feeling in the company that not everyone is aware of and sensitive to environmental imperatives and trade-offs, and that the opportunity costs of environmental quasi-resources (such as permits) are growing in significance to the company, is suggested below.

Recommendation 4: Develop communication and strategic planning tools along the lines of the analyses presented in Section 3.2 and quantify the impact of the scenarios in dollars and cents.

Finally, turning to motivation and control, it is clear from the discussion in Section 4 that the primary environment-driven imperative here is to get managers to anticipate, plan for, and do the things that must be done today to prepare for the future. The issue of accurately tracing costs and carrying out cost allocations for current performance reports is clearly not relevant here. Indeed, too great a focus on current financial performance can be dysfunctional for this purpose.

Recommendation 5: Identify a non-financial, goal-means hierarchy given a chosen strategic response to the longer-term environmental imperatives, communicate this through the organization, and set up appropriate performance metrics and incentive schemes to motivate desired actions.

VII.
ACCOUNTING FOR POLLUTION PREVENTION IN WASHINGTON STATE

By Christopher H. Stinson

1. Introduction

The companies described in these four case studies are all located in Washington State and subject to Pollution Prevention planning requirements. They provide a glimpse into the experience of companies compelled by law to take a closer look at their environmental costs. As they are all relatively small companies, with annual sales in the range of $10–$140 million, they provide additional insights into the special considerations for smaller firms.

For much of the 1980s, efforts to control industrial pollution centered on regulating the emission and disposal of pollutants from businesses. More recently, attention has been shifting to "pollution prevention" efforts that reduce the internal production of pollutants. Although many pollution prevention efforts are voluntary, many state (and even a few federal) authorities are requiring firms to demonstrate that they have investigated less polluting alternatives to their current waste-generating processes.

Currently, a wide range of requirements are imposed by different states. Some have no pollution prevention requirements at all; all pollution prevention efforts are essentially voluntary. Among states with some requirements, a range of regulations exist.

Washington State requires firms to identify sources of hazardous wastes at a detailed level of specific processes. This contrasts with the facility-level focus under federal emissions reporting (e.g., the Toxics Release Inventory or TRI), the product level

CASE HIGHLIGHTS: WASHINGTON STATE FIRMS

This collection of case studies looks at four relatively small firms in Washington, a state that requires companies to tabulate environmental costs as they prepare Pollution Prevention Plans. In quantifying the environmental savings, companies identify cost-effective projects that might otherwise have been overlooked.

At Heath Tecna, a manufacturer of composite materials for the aerospace industry, the value of lost raw material far exceeds the cost of disposal. Taken together, these costs supported a decision to invest in technology for increased materials efficiency. Management does not charge individual production units for off-site disposal costs to avoid short-term incentives for inappropriate waste disposal.

At Cascade Cabinet, a manufacturer of wood cabinets, the major environmental issues include solvents, volatile organic compounds, and wood waste. The company switched from a lacquer to varnish on environmental, safety, and cost grounds, and is converting wood scraps into a salable product, eliminating disposal costs.

Spectrum Glass manufactures stained sheet glass for art and architectural applications. A key environmental issue is the use of cadmium oxide, a highly toxic and hazardous chemical, as a colorant for ruby-red glass. Increasingly restrictive regulations on the manufacture of this chemical could lead to the disappearance of ruby-red glass in the near future.

Eldec Corporation designs and builds electronic equipment for aerospace applications. The accounting department was concerned that accounting systems might have to be modified to comply with the regulations. After preparing the plan, the company felt they benefited from the process. Department of Defense accounting standards may discourage revised accounting for environmental costs.

—The editors

(where business units typically estimate profitability), or the firm level (where financial data are commonly aggregated). Also, the firm must compare the costs (including environmental compliance costs) of current processes and cleaner alternatives. In Washington, the requirement was phased in over three years (first for the largest hazardous waste generators, and later for smaller generators). The Pollution Prevention Plan must include:

- a description of each process that generates hazardous wastes;
- a comparison of the costs of current processes and cleaner technologies;
- a description of the "environmental accounting system" used to collect environmental compliance costs; and,
- specific performance goals for reducing hazardous substance use, reducing hazardous wastes, and recycling materials.

Annual updates are required if there have been any changes in available technology, production processes, and so on since the original plan was filed. The Department of Ecology reviews the plan, and can reject it if it is incomplete. Each firm must file at least the plan's Executive Summary with the state (where the document becomes accessible to the public). Failure to file a required Pollution Prevention Plan can result in a fine of $1,000 or three times the firm's annual hazardous waste disposal fees, whichever is greater.

Several other states have added pollution prevention planning requirements to the existing landscape of environmental regulation. Additionally, there are federal requirements that touch on the accounting for environmental costs. Perhaps the most explicit language about this is contained in draft guidelines under the Resource Conservation and Recovery Act (RCRA):

B. *Characterization of Waste Generation and Waste Management Costs:* Maintain a waste accounting system to track the types and amounts of wastes as well as the types and amounts of the hazardous constituents in wastes... Additionally, a waste generator should determine the true costs associated with waste management and clean-up, including the costs of regulatory oversight compliance, paperwork and reporting requirements, loss of production potential, costs of materials found in the waste stream, (perhaps based on the purchase price of these materials), transportation/treatment/storage/disposal cost, employee exposure and health care, liability insurance, and possible future RCRA or Superfund corrective action costs. Both the volume and toxicities of generated hazardous wastes should be taken into account. Substantial uncertainty in calculating many of these costs, especially future liabilities, may exist. Therefore, each organization should find the best method to account for the true costs of waste management and cleanup.

D. *A Cost Allocation System:* Where practical and implementable, organizations should appropriately allocate the true costs of waste management to the activities responsible for generating the waste in the first place (e.g. identifying specific operations that generate the waste, rather than charging the waste management cost to "overhead"). Cost allocation can properly highlight the parts of the organization where the greatest opportunities for waste minimization exist; without allocating costs, waste minimization opportunities can be obscured by accounting practices that do not clearly identify the activities generating the hazardous wastes.

The four cases were not intended as a random sample of the undoubtedly varied experiences of firms under the pollution prevention requirements. Thus, it would be a mistake to judge the effectiveness of the program on the basis of these cases alone. Nonetheless, they do provide a glimpse into how some mid-sized firms have responded to this external requirement to account for some environmental costs.

2. Heath Tecna Aerospace

2.1. The Company, Its Products, and Its Markets
Heath Tecna Aerospace is a Kent, Washington corporation that manufactures a variety of parts for the aerospace industry. It was

acquired by Ciba-Geigy in January 1988 and is now part of their Composites Division. Heath Tecna has four divisions: Kent Structures, Kent Interiors, Bellingham Retrofit Interiors, and a new Wind Power division. Three divisions manufacture composite-material parts for the aerospace industry. Currently, Kent Structures produce radomes (radar-containing nose cones for commercial aircraft), fairings (units that improve the aerodynamic characteristics of the wing-body joint), and other structural components. The two Interior divisions produce interior sidewalls and overhead compartments for commercial aircraft. In 1989, nearly one-third of all active commercial plane interiors had been manufactured by Heath Tecna. The Wind Power division makes 50-foot windmill blades for wind power generators. This case focuses on the Kent Structures Division, as it is the primary generator of hazardous waste and air emissions.

Heath Tecna's products are sold to most of the major aerospace companies, including McDonald-Douglas, Lockheed, General Dynamics, and Boeing. The company has experienced a decline in business activity as a consequence of the worldwide slump in the aerospace industry. For example, there are currently about 1,000 employees, down from 1,600 in 1991. (Additionally, the Federal budget cutbacks in the A-6 program directly affect Heath Tecna, to the extent that some parts in production will not be finished.) Several competitors exist in the Pacific Northwest, and others are found throughout the United States. Consequently, there is substantial price competition for the jobs that Heath Tecna undertakes.

2.2. Manufacturing Process for Composite-Material Parts
The manufacturing process has eight main stages: tooling, kit-cutting, honeycomb, layup, autoclave, trimming/finishing, assembly, and painting. The tooling department makes the "tools," or forms, used in the layup department. The kit-cutting and honeycomb areas generate the materials used in the remainder of the production process. Workers in the kit-cutting area cut carefully measured patterns from sheets of resin-impregnated fabric by hand. This is in contrast to operations where the resin is worked into similar fabric on site, e.g., autobody shops. The pre-impregnated fabric (i.e., fab-

ric impregnated with resin before being received by Heath Tecna) or "prepreg" is purchased from another Ciba-Geigy-owned corporation in California. Workers in the honeycomb area carve honeycomb-configured paper into three-dimensional shapes and dip the final honeycomb into a phenolic resin to strengthen it. The resin-coated honeycomb is lighter than an equivalent volume of prepreg and is used where weight needs to be controlled.

The layup department is where the composite aerospace units are built. The sticky pieces of honeycomb and precut pieces of prepreg are layered onto tools (i.e., forms) and stuck together. These composite units are cured in large autoclaves where pressure and temperature are carefully controlled. After being autoclaved, the cured unit is taken to the trimming/finishing department, where excess material is trimmed from the unit and any surface imperfections are repaired. Other parts are fastened to the composite unit in the assembly area. Finally, finished units are taken to the painting department, where they receive coats of appropriate primers and paints.

2.3. Environmental Issues

Heath Tecna faces four main environmental issues. Its parent corporation is quite proactive regarding environmental issues and has adopted voluntary waste-reduction goals that affect the company's business decisions. Heath Tecna's local management is concerned about how they are perceived by their community and state. Also, the company faces explicit regulatory constraints on both the emission of hazardous chemicals into the atmosphere and the disposal of hazardous solid wastes.

Ciba-Geigy gives substantive guidance to Heath Tecna on environmental matters. For example, Ciba established two of the company's waste-reduction goals: cutting the generation of all wastes by 10 percent (mentioned in Heath Tecna's Pollution Prevention Plan), and reducing the generation of TRI wastes by 20 percent (as part of Ciba's voluntary participation in the Environmental Protection Agency's 33/50 Program). In September 1993, Ciba representatives completed an internal audit of Heath Tecna that evaluated several environmental issues, in addition to other, more traditional topics.

Heath Tecna also has its own commitment to deal with environmental issues before they become significant community or regulatory problems. Its goal is to be the employer of choice—and the corporate neighbor of choice—in Kent, Washington. There is a strong commitment from management to have employees feel that the company is a good one in a broad social sense. As a consequence, Heath Tecna has won awards and recognition for environmental awareness. The company started a waste-minimization program in 1988. In 1989, it had to apply to the city of Kent to build a chemical storage facility. During the permit process, the city announced that Heath Tecna would have to hire an outside consultant to help prepare a waste-minimization plan. When the company was able to demonstrate that it already had a waste-minimization program in place, it was able to prepare its own plan for the permit process (and save consulting fees).

The Environment and Safety Manager says that he has had no problems in receiving approval for waste-reduction techniques proposed to management. Many of these have actually proved to be cost-saving. For example, in the late 1980s a defoamer was added to a water-wash spray booth. Previously, the booth had to be cleaned once a month, but now Heath Tecna needs to clean it only once every three to four months. The payback from this (in reduced waste-disposal fees) was almost instantaneous.

Heath Tecna's primary air emissions are from evaporating solvents, mainly acetone and methyl ethyl ketone (MEK). In 1991, the company used 88,642 pounds of solvents in the manufacturing process. In the same year, it released about 60,000 pounds of acetone and MEK as air emissions; the remainder was discarded as hazardous solid or liquid waste. The Painting Department is a source of additional hazardous air pollutants. Heath Tecna can use only paints preapproved by the Puget Sound Air Pollution Control Agency (PSAPCA). However, approved paints are not necessarily without risk. For example, one European customer requires Heath Tecna to use a carcinogenic chromate-based primer. Even though PSAPCA allows this, company engineers are trying to persuade the customer to let Heath-Tecna use alternative (less carcinogenic) primers to minimize employee exposure to hazardous substances.

Prepreg waste contributed 170,000 pounds of the 320,000 pounds of product-related waste (hazardous and non-hazardous combined) generated at Heath Tecna in 1992. This resin-impregnated fabric is a hazardous material, and the waste pieces are hazardous waste. The kit-cutting area creates 90-95 percent of the prepreg waste and most of the hazardous waste generated. Approximately 35 percent of the fabric is not used when parts are cut out of sheets. Heath Tecna has installed one machine that will automate some of this process and hopes to decrease wastage to 25 percent.

The company is currently considering installing an electric oven to cure prepreg waste (at a capital cost of $20,000, plus $15,000 annually for operation and maintenance, plus one-third to one-half of a $40,000/year employee). The cured prepreg can be disposed of as a non-hazardous waste at a much lower cost. Currently, Heath Tecna spends approximately $85,000 annually to dispose of the waste, so this project presents some cost savings. In fact, because a rolled sheet of prepreg costs $22-$60 per linear yard, Heath Tecna is currently spending $85,000-$100,000 in waste-disposal costs to throw away "hazardous waste" that cost $5 million. Heath Tecna is also working with Battelle on the feasibility of a prepreg recycling program.

2.4. Accounting for Environmental Costs
Heath Tecna recently began charging each division for some environmental compliance costs. The 1994 budget cycle was the first year that the compliance office (with a $600,000 budget share) was not borne entirely by Kent Structures Division. In that year, $170,000 of the $600,000 expense was allocated to the overhead of the other divisions. However, Heath Tecna does not charge back waste disposal fees to different production groups because the firm does not want budget constraints to affect the behavior of process managers (e.g., Heath Tecna does not want to create a short-term incentive for improper waste disposal).

Information on waste disposal costs is not used in pricing and preparing bids. Heath Tecna estimates composite material efficiencies (which is then used to calculate the quantity of composite materials required). But direct environmental costs are not taken into consideration. This is at least partly because waste disposal fees are relatively small. Heath Tecna's 1990 gross sales were $138 million. In that same year, total environmental compliance costs were less than $500,000 (including $270,000 in disposal fees at the Kent divisions and $60,000 in disposal fees at the other two divisions). And the company probably had about $16 million in year-end inventory. Consequently, the potential cost savings from careful inventory management are much greater than are those from controlling waste disposal expenses. Nonetheless, it can still be worthwhile to monitor waste-disposal practices carefully.

Environmental considerations affect the compensation of several managers. Compensation for some senior executives depends in part on whether Heath Tecna meets the waste-reduction goals established by Ciba. Formerly, line supervisors were evaluated only on whether production goals were met. Now, production safety is also considered in their evaluation and compensation. This safety analysis includes not only a review of raw safety statistics, but also routine audits of each manager's compliance with company safety practices and policies by the Heath Tecna Safety Committee (and supplemental evaluation by the corporate audit team).

Finally, a Chemical Hazard and Regulatory Information System (CHRIS) is under development at Heath Tecna. This new computer system was inspired by concern for the exacting reports required under environmental, occupational and other laws. CHRIS is organized on a process-by-process basis; it will allow managers to review Heath Tecna's inventory twice a week, to determine the total levels of regulated components on site, and to compare those levels with the current EPA thresholds for reporting. This management tool will also have a hazardous materials communication unit that eventually will be graphics-oriented (and hence accessible to workers for whom English is not a first language). Although not strictly a cost-accounting system, CHRIS will allow Heath Tecna to monitor environmental compliance more closely than is currently possible.

2.5. The Pollution Prevention Plan and Its Effects
The Environment and Safety Manager supervised the preparation of Heath Tecna's 1992 Pollution Prevention Plan. This required 300 people from production to go through one hour of training each,

plus about 500 hours of engineering and administrative time, for a total cost of about $41,000.

Heath Tecna's Pollution Prevention Plan identifies 30 opportunities for reducing pollution and associated expenses; only 4 of these opportunities were rejected. In the manager's view, the plan helped formalize the company's waste-minimization program, but because Heath Tecna already had one in place, the Pollution Prevention Plan "hasn't helped put us anywhere faster." The plan per se apparently had little or no immediate benefit for the company. As noted, all production employees were required to undergo an hour of training during the Plan preparation. This certainly enhanced employee awareness of waste-creation and disposal issues, but Heath Tecna only complemented the already existing Solvent Safety Communications and Hazard Communications Programs.

Unlike some firms in Washington state, Heath Tecna was already considering the impact of many environmental compliance costs before the Pollution Prevention Plan was required. Consequently, the company probably gained relatively little from plan preparation per se, though the earlier analyses that contributed to the plan were certainly valuable. In addition, because of the earlier analysis, the plan was relatively inexpensive to prepare. Heath Tecna's experience will not be representative of other firms that are not as far along in their analysis of environmental costs.

3. Cascade Cabinet

3.1. The Company, Its Products, and Its Markets
Cascade Cabinet is a privately owned manufacturer of kitchen and bathroom wooden cabinets that are sold to contractors (through independent sales representatives), dealers (who resell to individuals), and the military (through bidding on military contracts). Gross sales are $14 million annually. Cascade's main markets are on the U.S. west coast, Hawaii, and Alaska, with some sales also going to Japan and extraterritorial U.S. military bases (e.g., Guam). Offering specialty cabinets gives Cascade Cabinet a marketing

edge over many of its competitors, which offer only a limited set of cabinet styles. The company has 200 employees at two facilities in Woodinville, Washington; about 180 employees work at the main facility. The owner, who resides in the eastern United States, has a strong, personal commitment to environmental issues. Managers at Cascade Cabinet describe their management style as a "learning partnership" with Cascade's employees. In addition to the president, three senior managers are in charge of accounting, production control, sales, and marketing. Because of Cascade's small size, there is no separate environmental department.

3.2. Manufacturing Process for Cabinets
Cabinets are assembled in batch jobs. For each order, wood is cut, shaped, sanded, and assembled. Next, the components are sent to the spray booth, where stain, sealant, and lacquer are applied. Components are carried through the spray booth on an overhead conveyer line. The application of stain, sealant, and lacquer releases volatile organic compounds (VOCs), most of which are captured by the spray booth air filters and some of which escape into the air. After drying, cabinet hardware is attached and the finished components are assembled into cabinets. Finally, the finished product is held for shipping to the customer.

If components need reworking because of poor quality spraying, they are diverted to a rework station, where they are stripped by hand and then returned to the spray booth. The stripping process generates spent solvents (i.e., thinners).

3.3. Environmental Issues
Cascade Cabinet faces three main environmental problems: air pollution, hazardous waste production, and non-hazardous solid-waste production.

First, as noted, the finishing process releases regulated VOCs into the air. According to their 1991 TRI report, approximately 136,000 pounds of hazardous chemical wastes (xylene, toluene, methyl isobutyl ketone, methanol, and methyl ethyl ketone) were released into the atmosphere. According to Cascade Cabinet's Pollution Prevention Plan, they used about 263,000 pounds of stains, sealer, and lacquer in 1991; thus, 51 percent of these hazardous products are released as air emissions.

The company's air-emission permits are issued by PSAPCA. Currently, to the company's disappointment, gross permit fees are increasing even though its emission levels have been declining. Cascade Cabinet pays $20 a ton for permitted VOC emissions.

Second, the rework station used 12,150 pounds of thinner in 1991; this generated about 6,000 pounds of spent solvent. That is, about 50 percent of the purchased thinner ends up as hazardous waste. A private hauler picks up about 200 gallons of hazardous, liquid waste every two to three months at a charge of $1,000 per trip (i.e., hazardous waste disposal costs are approximately $4,800/year). These wastes are transported off-site and either recycled or burned for energy recovery. In 1993, the hauler was able to recycle 43 percent of the liquid wastes (this creates a recycling credit, and a reduction in net reported generation of hazardous wastes, in the TRI reporting).

Third, the company generates non-hazardous wastes. The filters on the air-cleaning fans become clogged and are then sent to a landfill. The cardboard sheets that surround the spray-booth area are sent to a corrugated-cardboard recycler. In addition, Cascade generates 5,000–7,000 pounds of wood scrap per day. In the past, this solid waste was hauled to a local landfill every one to three days at a cost of $500 per truckload (i.e., approximately 200 loads a year at an annual cost of $100,000). This wood waste represents unused materials originally purchased for $25,000 per month. The landfill charge for wood waste has increased from $50 to $82.50 per ton. This increase led Cascade to invest $60,000 in setting up a large grinder to chip the wood waste. The chipped waste is now sold and shipped to an Oregon particle-board manufacturer. Now Cascade's only disposal expense is the one hour used each morning to grind up the wood waste from the previous day.

Finally, sawdust from Cascade's new sander is too fine to go to the particle-board manufacturer; it was originally burnt on site and is now used for fuel in a nearby wood-drying kiln at another company. In the future, this sawdust may be sent to a cogeneration unit that is being built by Scott Paper.

3.4. The Pollution Prevention Plan and Its Effects

Cascade has had a strong commitment to minimizing the generation of waste, though it does not expect to eliminate all waste. A Waste Management Team works toward a "zero-waste" goal. A manufacturing engineer is head of the Waste Management Team, which also prepared the Pollution Prevention Plan. He is also responsible for materials disposition (i.e., disposing of out-of-date products and obsolete hardware as economically as possible), dealing with special orders to Cascade Cabinet (i.e., design, pricing, and testing of special orders and trouble-shooting production problems with these orders). The other team members include the finishing supervisor (who knows materials well), the vice-president of engineering, the owner, and the human resource manager (who also provides backup on form-filling compliance for the head of the team and is responsible for emergency spill response).

The Pollution Prevention Plan submitted by Cascade Cabinet is unusual because all the technologically and cost-feasible waste-reduction opportunities described had already been implemented before the plan was prepared. Cascade Cabinet had not only implemented several internal pollution prevention programs, they had also requested one of their stain suppliers to develop a high-quality, water-based stain. Although the plan preparation per se apparently did not lead to the discovery of any new pollution prevention opportunities, it facilitated the organization of existing information and let the company examine its waste management practices. The head of the Waste Management Team feels very strongly that plan preparation was beneficial to the company.

Since the Plan was prepared, Cascade has shifted from nitrocellulose lacquer to conversion varnish. This contains fewer VOCs, is not hazardous, and costs only marginally more per area covered. Perhaps most important, the residual dust from this varnish is not explosive; a $1 million fire started in 1992 when a welding spark blew onto a lacquer dust pile. Thus, the new varnish lowers accident probabilities, has resulted in lower PSAQCB permit fees, and has saved money on insurance (because of the lowered explosion hazard).

Because of this and other pollution prevention activities, Cascade Cabinet achieved a 17-percent reduction in its 1993 hazardous waste production over the 1992 figure. In addition, they have dropped from five reportable TRI chemicals to four (due to the switch from the nitrocellulose lacquer).

3.5. Accounting for Environmental Costs

Production meetings are held at the start of each day. This provides a chance to inform managers about new changes and provides quick dissemination of new information. The accounting function in Cascade Cabinet is almost exclusively that of bookkeeping (instead of also having a proactive informational role). When members of management need information, the accounting staff assists in collecting the desired data. A monthly accounting report is distributed to all departments, reporting on the previous month's progress.

The company records the waste-production costs associated with each step of the manufacturing process. However, these expenses are only about 3.5 percent of total costs. Consequently, it is not surprising that no attempt is made to differentially charge these costs to different batch jobs.

Similarly, waste management is not explicitly considered in employee performance evaluations. However, there is at least one indirect way that waste management practices affect employee performance reviews. A training film on finishing techniques demonstrates how to minimize waste of finishing compounds. Employees are subsequently evaluated on how well they follow the techniques in which they were trained.

4. Spectrum Glass

4.1. The Company, Its Products, and Its Markets

Spectrum Glass is a privately owned company that manufactures about 30 percent of the world's specialty sheet glass (i.e., colored sheet glass for stained-glass windows or lamps). Spectrum is a high-volume, low-margin producer with about $12 million in annual sales. Most (50-60 percent) sales are to the stained glass market (e.g., arts and crafts shops, stained glass artists, etc.). The remainder are to overseas manufacturers of specialty lighting who receive the shipped glass, produce lighting products, and ship the finished products back to the United States. Although there are other manufacturers of specialty sheet glass in North America, Spectrum (with 160 employees) is substantially larger than any of its competitors.

Spectrum uses both daytanks (where melting, cooking, and usage take place in a 24-hour cycle) and continuous furnaces (where molten glass is removed at the same rate that raw materials are added). The latter process produces glass that withstands more stress than other sheet glass. Continuous furnaces require large amounts of electricity. The company can afford this because of the relatively low price of electricity in the Pacific Northwest. Continuous furnaces also require a substantial investment in equipment. These high upfront and operating costs keep many of Spectrum's smaller competitors from investing in similar equipment, giving the company a competitive advantage. Apparently, the limited size of the worldwide market keeps better capitalized firms from entering this market.

4.2. Manufacturing Specialty Sheet Glass

Spectrum manufactures its specialty glass on a batch basis in a plant built in 1979. For each production run, sand, soda ash, limestone and coloring chemicals are mixed together. Because some of the colorants are hazardous, they are mixed in a closed weighing room with a measured volume of glass cullet and put into an electric furnace. Furnace smoke and weighing room dust are vented to a baghouse (i.e., a room separated from the plant by a series of fabric filters that help separate solid particulates from the air).

After the furnace melts the glass and oxidizes the colorants, the new sheet glass is formed, cooled, and removed from the furnace. If the glass is broken during cooling or subsequent handling, it is crushed into cullet. Sometimes this cullet is recycled through the furnace; however, it is not always possible to reuse cullet (e.g., the original mix may have included some chemicals that changed composition when they were heated).

After manufacture, the finished glass is cut into desired dimensions and packed for shipping. Because the glass must be well protected during shipping, about one-tenth of Spectrum's product cost is for packaging. Any remaining glass fragments are crushed into cullet and recycled or sold.

4.3. Environmental Issues

Cadmium oxide and other pigments used in the manufacture of yellow, orange, and red glass are highly toxic, hazardous chemicals. For the past 90 years, both glaze and glass producers have searched—unsuccessfully, to date—for alternative, less toxic pigments. Spectrum Glass is one of only two U.S. manufacturers still making ruby-red glass; because of environmental concerns, this red glass is no longer made in Europe. Consequently, even mosques in North Africa now buy their red window glass from Spectrum.

The coloring chemicals are the primary source of the two environmental issues—hazardous wastes and air emissions—facing Spectrum Glass. For example, increasingly restrictive regulations on the manufacture of cadmium oxide will probably lead to the disappearance of ruby-red glass in the near future. Asarco (in Tacoma, Washington), Spectrum Glass's biggest supplier of cadmium oxide, has discontinued this product; other manufacturers are apparently also considering this move. Alternatively, some manufacturers are moving their cadmium production out of the United States where they melt the cadmium into glass, crush it, and ship the crushed glass back to their U.S. customers.

In the early 1990s, Spectrum Glass was in discussions with regulators regarding the "visible plume" from their stack. By 1992, the technical staff realized that their operations would be limited by additional regulatory constraints regarding air emissions. Currently, Spectrum faces the same regulations as non-specialty glass manufacturers—that is, limits on the particulates in air emissions without regard for their toxicity. However, more restrictive emission requirements of cadmium are pending from the PSAQCB. In anticipation of these new regulations, Spectrum Glass has undertaken stack sampling of its air emissions.

In response to stack sampling, Spectrum installed the baghouse, where most toxic particulates from the weighing room and furnace are recaptured. Currently, the baghouse captures 99.7 percent of the material previously emitted into the air. This is the "best available technology," but Spectrum will be out of compliance if more advanced technologies are required in the future.

Hazardous solid wastes are produced when cadmium burns off during the manufacturing process and is captured as ash in the stack. Hazardous wastes are also generated from spilling and wastage that ends up on the plant floor. However, not all glass breakage becomes hazardous waste. For example, Spectrum's white glass cullet is sold to a marble manufacturer who makes "industrial marbles" for mixing the paint stored inside cans of spray paint.

Until mid-1993, Spectrum had been shipping its cadmium wastes to an Oregon landfill. But this landfill recently closed its gates to such wastes. Now, the company trucks them to a waste processor in Arkansas. It could also mix the cadmium wastes (in the ash from the stacks) with melted glass (leaving the hazardous materials unable to leach, percolate, and so on from the encasing glass), but this would probably require Spectrum to undergo lengthy and expensive regulatory review as a Treatment, Storage, and Disposal Facility. Currently, the company does melt floor sweepings into glass that is then crushed and sold for use in roads and driveways. (Because this glass is sold, these materials are not classified as a hazardous "waste".)

4.4. The Pollution Prevention Plan and Its Effects

Spectrum Glass' Pollution Prevention Plan was prepared by the environmental compliance engineer, who was hired for this task in July 1992. He solicited employee input, attempting to make them feel like they "owned" the project. The risk estimates in the plan were made after talking with workers about accident rates, reviewing toxicology data in reference texts, reviewing health and safety records, and so on.

The Pollution Prevention Plan was submitted at the end of August 1992. It documented the waste management programs in place and forced management to think directly about these issues. All waste-reduction projects described in the plan were under way even before the plans were required by the state. However, specific waste reduction goals were reviewed and approved by management as part of the plan preparation. Additional suggestions (e.g., switching to solid pallets from slatted pallets to keep bags from being ripped open by fork lifts) were received when the plan was discussed with workers. As a consequence, top management became aware of some issues and suggestions for changes for the first time when they reviewed the plan.

4.5. Accounting for Environmental Costs

Although ruby-red glass generates more hazardous wastes than other colors, Spectrum does not differentiate environmental costs for the different glasses. Nor does it charge more for the ruby-red glass. In part, this is because the continuous manufacturing process mixes "fines" (i.e., fine ash collected from cloth filters in the baghouse) from the different glasses. Spectrum generates about 15,300 pounds of "fines" annually as well as an additional 2,700 pounds of other hazardous waste. The company pays approximately $3,500 per ton (about $32,500 a year) to dispose of the fines and other hazardous waste.

Spectrum does price some products higher because their direct manufacturing costs are higher, e.g., when coloring chemicals are more volatile, less stable, etc. However, these higher prices reflect only additional direct material and direct labor costs. Under the current regulations controlling the production of cadmium wastes, Spectrum can continue to mix ruby-red and other glass production. If cadmium use becomes prohibitively expensive, ruby-red glass may well be dropped from Spectrum's production.

5. Eldec Corporation

5.1. The Company, Its Products, and Its Markets

Eldec Corporation is a public corporation that designs and manufactures electronic and electro-mechanical instruments for commercial and defense aerospace applications. It is the world's leading supplier of proximity switches that monitor the status of critical airplane systems. Eldec has about 1,100 employees working in four divisions at Martha Lake and one division in Bothell, Washington near Seattle. The Monitor & Control Division has 200 employees. The Aircraft Systems Division (in Bothell) has 500 employees. The Power Conversion Division has 200 employees. The Central Services Division includes the machine shop and has 150 employees; this division is not a profit center. The remaining employees are in the Corporate Division.

5.2. Manufacturing Electronic Instruments

Eldec manufactures fuel-flow controls (Monitor & Control Division), power conversion units (Power Conversion Division), and monitoring units for hydraulic and other airplane systems (Aircraft Systems Division). The company also conducts research for product improvement (e.g., the Monitor & Control Division has a Fuel Flow Laboratory). In addition, the Central Services Division holds a machine shop and is the source of all internally manufactured printed wire boards.

Eldec gets 55 percent of its revenues from commercial sales and the other 45 percent from contracts (or subcontracts) with the U.S. Department of Defense (DoD). With the recent decline in business activity in both commercial aerospace and the defense industry, Eldec has laid off 25 percent of its employees in the last four years; in the same period, sales have dropped by 20 percent.

5.3. Environmental Issues

The diverse set of manufacturing processes at Eldec requires the use of many hazardous substances (e.g., solvents) and creates some hazardous waste. Eldec's defense contracts limit disclosure of how most of these compounds are used (or generated).

A second problem involves analysis of contingent liabilities due to pre-existing hazardous wastes at newly purchased facilities. Recently, Eldec acquired Venus, a Long Island, New York, manufacturer of high-voltage electronics. Environmental issues were very important considerations in this transaction. Venus had leased their current manufacturing site for 13 months prior to the purchase. Because Venus was owned by a U.K. parent corporation, Eldec was concerned about its own exposure to hazardous waste at the Long Island site from pre-purchase activities. Any pre-purchase liability associated with Venus's activity at this site might fall on Eldec if, for example, the British parent sold all its U.S. operations.

To address these concerns, Eldec did a Phase I survey of the Long Island site as part of due diligence early in the negotiation process; they did a Phase II survey of the site prior to signing the acquisition contract; and they plan to do a Phase II replicate sampling when they leave the Long Island site in an attempt to limit their liability for cleanup there. Finally, Eldec was able to include a small holdback in the purchase agreement, although this was substantially smaller than Eldec's potential liability for site cleanup.

5.4. The Pollution Prevention Plan and Its Effects

Eldec's Pollution Prevention Plan was due at the Washington State Department of Ecology in September 1992. Because of the many business pressures competing for managers' time, the original plan submission was rejected as inadequate by the Department. Eldec was granted an extension and submitted a complete Pollution Prevention Plan in 1993. The final plan was prepared by a facilities engineer in the Corporate Division, who worked full time on it for six months with an engineering co-op student.

Different corporate departments had different initial reactions to the required Plan preparation. For example, Purchasing viewed this as an opportunity to obtain better control over hazardous-substance inventory and suppliers. But the Accounting department originally did not support doing more than was minimally necessary because of confusion regarding whether their existing accounting systems would have to be modified to comply with the regulations. This confusion was not unreasonable. Eldec's corporate accounting supervisor was on the original Department of Ecology workgroup where some regulators had proposed having firms demonstrate that their financial accounting systems—as opposed to their cost accounting systems—traced all environmental compliance costs. Because GAAP do not require such tracing, this would have been quite expensive for Eldec. Nonetheless, when the final Plan was completed, all departments felt its preparation had been a useful exercise.

The Pollution Prevention Plan gave Eldec an opportunity to search for environmental cost savings at a time when industry cutbacks were attracting much of management's attention. Although the company had undertaken earlier pollution prevention projects (e.g., reductions in the use of ozone-depleting substances were under way), these activities had not been coordinated previously. In preparing the plan, "process owners" (i.e., process supervisors or process engineers who did not necessarily have profit/loss responsibility for the specific process) were identified. Information on process flow and waste generation (from a database assimilated from manifests, invoices, and other information from the compliance manager) was given to the process owners to use during pollution-prevention brain-storming sessions with their coworkers.

Preparing the plan specifically led Eldec to examine many subprocesses that otherwise might have been overlooked until later. For example, an ad hoc rule determining the frequency of preventative maintenance for some machinery was replaced with a statistical control technique that reduced the frequency of preventative maintenance (and the accompanying use of hazardous solvents). In addition, the printed-wire-board manufacturing process was changed so that a hazardous sludge was reduced by over 60 percent. Interestingly, this information was available earlier, but had not been acted on until the plan-preparation process focused the attention of the process owners on the opportunity (and perhaps empowered them to seize it). Some potential pollution prevention opportunities have been constrained by military specifications required for some of Eldec's products. For cost and control reasons, Eldec's commercial processes are usually considered to be the same as their military processes.

Eldec plans to continue to use pollution prevention methodologies in the future. The team responsible for plan preparation (and their supervisors) feel strongly that the exercise was cost-effective and had a positive payback for the company. The Accounting department now also feels the plan was worthwhile both from a narrow, first-order economic perspective and from a broader perspective incorporating Eldec's commitment to minimizing its environmental impact.

5.5. Accounting for Environmental Costs

The Monitor & Control, Power Conversion, and Aircraft Systems Divisions are each profit centers; the Central Services and Corporate Divisions are cost centers. Until 1990, all overhead costs were charged back to each division on the basis of square footage. In 1991, Eldec started charging back disposal costs to "manufacturing overhead" for each of the three profit centers as well as for each of three manufacturing areas within Central Services, and to individual manufacturing areas within each division (i.e., tracing costs and not charging on the basis of square footage). Eldec spends a total of about $150,000 a year on hazardous waste disposal, about 0.15 percent of 1992 net sales. Assignable permitting fees, effluent analysis costs, and employee training expenses are also charged back to each division, but environmental training is not treated any differently than other training.

The Plan preparation encouraged two changes to Eldec's control system. One change will include hazardous waste production statistics in a quarterly financial report for senior management. In addition, the inventory system is changed so that chemicals can be flagged if they create "hazardous waste," create "extremely hazardous waste," or are "likely to be classified as hazardous in the future." This information eventually will be incorporated both into an activity-based costing system and into a system for generating TRI reports.

Because Eldec has to comply with the Department of Defense Accounting Standards for its defense contracts, it is often difficult to make substantive changes to their accounting methods, such as changing whether environmental compliance costs are allocated or traced. This difficulty arises because Eldec has to file a cost impact statement any time a change in accounting methods is made. If the change results in costs being assigned to government (not commercial) projects that are lower than the bid costs, Eldec has to refund the difference. If the change results in higher costs, however, DoD does not increase what they pay Eldec.

In one example of this, Eldec had been assigning all phone costs at a high level (e.g., division), and started allocating those costs on the basis of certain input costs. As a result, they had to make an $85,000 refund to DoD because of the way cost allocations changed. (The Aircraft System Division was 80 percent commercial and the Power Conversion Division was 90 percent defense; costs shifted between these divisions.) As a consequence, Eldec looks for offsetting accounting changes that they can implement simultaneously. If there is no net effect, the changes can be implemented without adversely affecting the company. Thus, these DoD standards create a disincentive to implementing changes in how environmental costs are accounted for.

About the Authors

Dr. R. Darryl Banks is Director of the Technology and Environment Program at the World Resources Institute in Washington, D.C.

Ms. Beth Beloff is Director of the Institute for Corporate Environmental Management at the University of Houston in Texas.

Dr. Daryl Ditz is an Associate in the Technology and Environment Program at the World Resources Institute in Washington, D.C.

Dr. Miriam Heller is an Assistant Professor of Industrial Engineering at the University of Houston in Texas.

Dr. Devaun Kite is an Assistant Professor of Accounting at the University of Houston in Texas.

Dr. Ajay Maindiratta is an Associate Professor of Accounting at New York University in New York City.

Ms. Janet Ranganathan is a Research Analyst in the Technology and Environment Program at the World Resources Institute in Washington, D.C.

Dr. David Shields is an Associate Professor of Accounting at the University of Houston in Texas.

Dr. Christopher Stinson is an Assistant Professor of Accounting at the University of Texas at Austin.

Dr. Rebecca Todd is a Professor of Accounting at Boston University in Massachusetts.

About WRI

The World Resources Institute is a research and policy organization helping governments, the private sector, environmental and development organizations, and others address a fundamental question: How can societies meet human needs and nurture economic growth while preserving the natural resources and environmental integrity on which life and economic vitality ultimately depend?

WRI's books and reports present accurate information about global resources and environmental conditions, analyses of emerging issues, and creative yet workable policy responses. To deepen public understanding, the institute also undertakes briefings, seminars, and conferences and offers material for use in print and broadcast media.

In developing countries, WRI provides field services and technical support for governments and non-governmental organizations working to ensure the sustainable use of natural resources.

ORDER NOW

and receive a 10% discount

__ YES, please send me _____ copies of **Green Ledgers: Case Studies in Corporate Environmental Accounting**, edited by Daryl Ditz, Janet Ranganathan, and R. Darryl Banks
ISBN: 1-56973-032-6
193 pages
$19.95, plus $3.50 shipping and handling

Ship to:

Name: _____

Address: _____

City, State, Zip Code: _____

Daytime Phone: _____

Billing Information:

___ Check enclosed in the amount of: $_____
___ Please charge my credit card: ____ Visa   ____ MasterCard

Account Number:_____

Expiration Date: _____

Signature: _____

In a hurry? Order by phone with a Visa or MasterCard by calling 1-800-822-0504, or 410-516-6963.

__ Please check here if you would like to receive a complete catalog of WRI publications. All orders must be prepaid. Prices subject to change without notice.

Return this form with payment, to: WRI Publications, P.O. Box 4852, Hampden Station, Baltimore, MD 21211.